SECRETS
of Louisville Chefs

MORE THAN 100 GREAT RECIPES
PLUS CULINARY TIPS FROM THE PROS

Published by Tobe Publishing, Inc., Louisville, Kentucky
Copyright (c) 2003 by Tobe Publishing and Nancy Miller

Secrets of Louisville Chefs
may be purchased for business
or promotional use or for special sale.

For information, please contact:

Tobe Publishing
2031 Nelson Miller Parkway, Suite 100
Louisville, KY 40223
502-245-6100
E-mail: jtobe@tobedirect.com

Designed by Julie Magee, three•sixty designs, LLC.
Cover photograph by Chris Witzke

ACKNOWLEDGMENTS

When I returned to Louisville after living in New York for 18 years, I was delighted to find that Louisville had become home to a deliciously diverse array of restaurants. During the past two years, I have had the pleasure of working with and getting to know many of our city's chefs. Their talent is extraordinary and the zeal with which they practice their craft and art is inspiring.

Secrets of Louisville Chefs celebrates their creativity and accomplishments. In this book, 36 of Louisville's top chefs graciously and generously share their recipes and secrets so that home cooks can recreate culinary masterpieces in their own kitchens. I thank each of the chefs for making this book a reality.

Secrets of Louisville Chefs would not have become this reality without John Tobe, of Tobe Publishing. Thank you, John, for having confidence in the book and in me.

I extend special thanks to Michael Lattin, of The Home Zone and the *Secrets of Louisville Chefs* television program, for inviting me to be part of such an exciting project.

Julie Magee, of three•sixty designs, you made the book look as great as the recipes taste. Thanks so much for your artistic vision.

Angela Dooley, I appreciate your considerable skills and your remarkable patience.

My thanks also go to Chris Witzke, of Premise Studio, for the cover photograph.

John Johnson, of The Wine Rack, thanks so much for contributing your expertise to this book.

Larry Hollingsworth, I thank you for your true Southern charm and for your hospitality in offering The Oakroom as the setting for our cover photo shoot. (And, the Champagne was a welcome surprise).

Thanks also to Michelle Ray for keeping the book organized and on track.

To Dan Crutcher and Bruce Allar, of Louisville magazine, I thank you for giving me the chance to work with you and to first meet some of the chefs featured in this book.

To Dottie Miller, my mother, thanks for being so supportive and so good at doing what a mother is supposed to do: think whatever her daughter does is great.

Thank you, Susan Crook, for your unique perspective on everything.

Just as dessert is often the last and best part of a meal, I've saved the last and most special thanks for Alex, my son. Thanks for eating so much take-out even though I was working on a cookbook about wonderful food. Thanks for maintaining your sense of humor when I was humorless. Thanks for being in a good mood, even when my mood was not so good. Most of all, thank you for being with me every day.

.Nancy Miller

CONTENTS

 Appetizers

Artemesia
Seared Foie Gras with Port, Cranberry Reduction and Caramelized Apples 3

Asiatique
Char-Broiled Balsamic Portobello with Strawberry-Garlic Sauce 4
Spicy Salmon Tartare Japonaise 5

Avalon
Avocado Hummus with Toasted Pita and Tomato 6

Azalea Restaurant
Tuna Tartare Napoleon with Avocado, Yellow Tomato and Crab Meat 7

Baxter Station Bar and Grill
Brie Salad...8

Bristol Bar and Grille
Artichoke Fritters 9

Buck's
Smoked Salmon with Burgundy Onions and Dill Mayonnaise 10

Café Metro
Tempura Fried Prawns with Blue Cornmeal and Cilantro Lime Aioli 11

Club Grotto American Bistro
Bacon Wrapped Scallops with Corn Fritters and Beurre Blanc.............................12

El Mundo
Avocado and Goat Cheese Quesadilla with Green Onion 13

The English Grill in the Camberley Brown Hotel
Steamer Clams with Country Ham, Garlic, Tomatoes and Parsley.............................14

Equus Restaurant/Jack's Lounge
Equus Shrimp Jenkins 15

Greek Paradise Café
Pandaisia 16

Jack Fry's Restaurant
Diver Scallops with Kentucky Bibb Lettuce and Black Truffle Oil.............................17

Jicama Grill
Shrimp Ceviche 18

Le Relais
Dungeness Crabcakes with Butternut Squash Purée and Citrus Beurre Blanc 19

Lilly's and La Pêche
Crab Garlic Custard on Organic Spinach with Warm Bacon Dressing................................20

Lynn's Paradise Café
Black Bean Chili 21

Porcini Restaurant
Granchio Torcello (Crab Cakes)..22

Restaurante The Mayan Gypsy
Black Bean Cakes..23

Salsa South Beach
Chicken and Green Chili Wontons with Ginger/Soy Dipping Sauce.................................24

Shariat's
Individual Roasted Exotic Mushroom and Root Vegetable Tartlets 25

Steam---Fire & Ice
Salmon Spread 26

The Flagship at the Galt House Hotel and Suites
Tomato Bisque with White Bean Relish and Parmigiano-Reggiano 27

The Oakroom at The Seelbach Hilton Louisville
Peppered Wild Mushroom Cappuccino 28

The Palmer Room at Lake Forest Country Club
Seared Sea Bass with Hazelnut Vinaigrette with Exotic Field Greens 29

The Patron Restaurant
Roasted Yellow Beet Salad with Cranberry Vinaigrette..30

211 Clover Lane
Seared Foie Gras with a Pear Semillon Coulis and Aged Balsamic 31

Uptown Café
Bacon-Wrapped Sea Scallops and Portobello Mushrooms 32

Vincenzo's
Tortino De Melenzane Con Risotto E Funghetti Di Bosco 33
(Eggplant Torte Filled with Risotto and Wild Mushrooms)

Winston's Restaurant at Sullivan University
Shrimp Madagascar with Wilted Spinach...34

Entrées

Artemesia
Sautéed Mahi-Mahi on Arugula with Scallop-Lobster Tortellini
and Roasted Pepper Dressing 37

Asiatique
Grilled Curry Glazed Wahoo, Sautéed Baby Bok Choy and
Mango+Strawberry Chutney 39

August Moon Chinese Bistro
Braised Baby Bok Choy with Shitake Mushrooms and Fresh Garlic 40
General's Chicken 41

Avalon
Beer and Chile Braised Boneless Short Ribs..42

Azalea Restaurant
Beef Tenderloin Stuffed with Wild Mushrooms and Goat Cheese 43

Baxter Station Bar and Grill
Tri-Colored Tortellini with Chipotle Basil Cream Sauce 44

Bristol Bar & Grille
Pork Loin Dijonaise 45

Buck's
Trout with Almond Flour Dijonaise..46

Café Metro
Roasted Leg of Lamb Stuffed with Wild Mushrooms and Escarole 47

Club Grotto American Bistro
Roast Breast of Chicken with Andouille-Cornbread Stuffing and
Apple Cider Glaze 48

El Mundo
Red Snapper al Mojo de Ajo and Soft Tacos with Mango Salsa 49

The English Grill in the Camberley Brown Hotel
Roasted Loin of Lamb with Hominy Grits 50

Equus Restaurant/Jack's Lounge
Chipotle Rubbed Mahi-Mahi with Chorizo, Corn and Purple Potato Hash 51

Greek Paradise Café
Moussaka 52

Jack Fry's Restaurant
Jack Fry's Pork Chop 53

Jicama Grill
Feijoada (Brazilian Black Bean and Meat Stew) 54
Churrascos De Argentina 56

Le Relais
Calvados and Tarragon Pork Tenderloin Medallions with Fingerling Potato Salad 57
Roasted Prawns in Lobster Broth Reduction 58

Lilly's and La Pêche
Slow-Roasted Lamb Shanks with Mediterranean Sauce and Creamy Grits with Chevre......59

Lynn's Paradise Café
Chicken Kentuckian 60

Porcini
Osso Bucco 61

Restaurante The Mayan Gypsy
Salmon Tikin Xik..62

Salsa South Beach
Rum Marinated Pork Chop with Banana Chutney 63

Shariat's
Duck Breast with Pomegranate Walnut Sauce 64

Steam---Fire & Ice
Pork Chops and Apple Sauce 65

The Flagship at the Galt House Hotel and Suites
Sautéed Grouper with Braised Napa Cabbage and Shitake Soy Glaze 66

The Oakroom at The Seelbach Hilton Louisville
Roasted Rack of Lamb 67

The Palmer Room at Lake Forest Country Club
Fresh Mozzarella and Prosciutto Stuffed French Veal Chop with Morel Marsala Sauce 68

The Patron Restaurant
Braised Chicken with Local Organic Mushrooms 69

211 Clover Lane
Cioppino 211 70

Uptown Café
Spicy Grilled Quail Wrapped with Zucchini with Marinated Grilled Asparagus
and Smoked Gouda Corncakes 71

Vincenzo's
Bocconcini De Vitello (Roulade of Veal) 73

Winston's Restaurant at Sullivan University
Stir Fry of Veal with Enoki Mushrooms, Peapods and Torn Pasta 74

Desserts

Asiatique
Malaysian Style Tapioca Pearls with Honeydew 77

Avalon
Individual Fried Apple Cheesecakes 78

Baxter Station Bar and Grill
Peaches and Cream 79

Bristol Bar & Grille
French Bread Pudding with Bourbon Sauce 80

Buck's
Key Lime Pie 81

Café Metro
Banana Poppyseed Guggelhopf 82

El Mundo
El Mundo's Flan 83

The English Grill in the Camberley Brown Hotel
Bourbon Chocolate Pecan Tart 84

Equus Restaurant/Jack's Lounge
Chocolate Orbit 85

Greek Paradise Café
Baklava 86

Jack Fry's Restaurant
Key Lime White Chocolate Mousse Torte with Blackberry Sauce 87

Lilly's and La Pêche
Pumpkin Cheesecake 88

Lynn's Paradise Café
Bourbon Ball French Toast 89

Porcini
Italian Cream Cake 90

Shariat's
White Chocolate Pumpkin Cheesecake 91

Steam---Fire & Ice
Too Easy Chocolate Mousse with Bourbon Caramel 92

Sweet Surrender
Banana Caramel Cake 93
Flourless Truffle Torte 94
White Chocolate Mousse Torte with Oreo Cookie Crust..................95

The Oakroom at The Seelbach Hilton Louisville
Malted Coffee Ice Cream 96

The Palmer Room at Lake Forest Country Club
Heavenlies 97

The Patron Restaurant
Buttermilk Panna Cotta with Quince and Apple Compote 98

211 Clover Lane
Chocolate and Banana Dacquoise with Appleton Rum Anglaise 99

Uptown Café
Créme Brûlée with Fresh Raspberries...100

Vincenzo's
Individual Chocolate Bombes 101

Winston's Restaurant at Sullivan University
Belgian Waffle De-Lite..102

Chefs' Secrets
Louisville's star chefs offer advice and share their secrets so that you can create
culinary magic in your own kitchen. 103

Pairing Food and Wine
John Johnson, owner of The Wine Rack, in Louisville, shares his experience and
insight on the multi-faceted subject of food and wine pairing. 137

About The Restaurants 143

Index 147

NOTE: Many of the dishes featured in Secrets of Louisville Chefs *include more than one recipe, including recipes that may be used in other appetizers, entrées and desserts.*

Appetizers

Traditionally, appetizers have been served to "stimulate the appetite at the beginning of the meal". But, appetizers can be the most tempting course of the meal. In these recipes the chefs imaginatively blend colors, flavors and textures so that the appetizer not only stimulates the appetite, but can be the star of the meal.

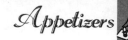

ARTEMESIA
Chef Stephen Young

Seared Foie Gras with Port, Cranberry Reduction and Caramelized Apples

This dish was first created for *Great Chefs of the World* on the Discovery Channel.

Serves 4

Port-Cranberry Reduction
1 cup ruby port
8 cups red grape juice
1 cup dried cranberries

Garnishes
1 leek, cleaned
Canola oil for deep-fat frying
4 scallions, tops only, cleaned

Apple Rings
1 cup unsalted butter
1/2 cup sugar
2 apples, cored

Goose
12 ounces fresh foie gras (goose or duck)
(available at specialty food markets)
Flour for dusting
Salt and freshly ground white pepper to taste
1/4 cup melted butter

To make the sauce: Combine port, grape juice and cranberries in a medium saucepan and cook over medium heat until reduced to a syrup, 10 to 15 minutes. Remove from heat.

To prepare the garnishes: Remove outer leaves from the leek and cut the center into very fine julienne. Heat the oil to 360 degrees in a deep fryer or deep saucepan and place about a fourth of the leek julienne in the fryer; do not crowd the pan. Fry for 15 seconds; drain leeks on paper towels. Repeat with remaining leeks. Bring a large saucepan of water to a rolling boil and add the scallions. Cook for 30 to 45 seconds; remove and place in cold water to stop the cooking. Remove and drain on paper towels.

To prepare the apple rings: Use an apple corer to core apples. Slice the apples into 1" thick rings. Melt the butter and sugar in a large sauté pan or skillet over medium high heat and add the apple rings. Sauté until caramelized and softened, 3 to 5 minutes. Remove from heat. You will use the 8 largest rings; remaining rings may be saved for another use, such as dessert.

To cook the foie gras: Cut or separate the foie gras into 8 pieces. Dust the foie gras with flour, shaking off the excess, and season with salt and pepper. Heat a large seasoned cast iron skilled over medium high heat until a drop of water turns to steam immediately when dropped on the surface. Add the melted butter and foie gras and sear for one minute per side. Drain on paper towels, patting the top side gently to remove any butter.

To serve: Place an apple ring in the center of each plate. Put a slice of foie gras on top of each ring. Top with another apple ring and another slice of foie gras. Pour the sauce over and around the foie gras and apples. Coil a blanched scallion and place on top of one of the foie gras slices. Top with flash-fried leek "hay." Repeat with remaining plates.

Char-Grilled Balsamic Portobello with Strawberry-Garlic Sauce

Serves 4

4 small fresh portobello mushrooms
1 cup organic baby field mix
1/2 cup olive oil
1/4 cup balsamic vinegar
2 sprigs rosemary, minced
1/2 clove garlic, minced
3 tablespoons sugar
1 tablespoon sesame oil
1/2 cup strawberries, sliced
1/2 cup Asiatique Stir Fry Sauce

For Balsamic glaze: In a food processor, blend rosemary, 1/2 clove of the garlic, sesame oil and sugar until well blended. Add balsamic vinegar and blend well. Slowly pour olive oil into processor until emulsified.

For Strawberry-Garlic Sauce: Place strawberries in a non-reactive bowl. In a sauté pan, simmer Asiatique Stir Fry Sauce and the remaining clove of minced garlic. When mixture boils, add sugar and stir until it caramelizes on the side of the pan. Pour the liquid into the fruit and stir.

To assemble each serving: Grill mushrooms 3 to 5 minutes on each side, brushing a little glaze on each side. Remove and cut into thin slices. Place 1/4 cup field mix in the middle of a plate and place the grilled portobello over the salad mix. Drizzle the strawberry-garlic sauce around the plate. Serve immediately.

ASIATIQUE
Chef Peng S. Looi

Spicy Salmon Tartare Japonaise

Serves 4

1/2 pound fresh Pacific salmon, diced
1/2 cucumber, seeded and diced
1 tablespoon pickled ginger, minced
3 chives, minced
1/2 red pepper, diced
1/2 tablespoon tobiko
(available in Korean or Japanese markets)
Salt and pepper to taste
Vietnamese hot chili garlic sauce to taste
(available in Korean or Japanese markets)
1/2 teaspoon mayonnaise
Dash sesame oil

Mix all ingredients well. Refrigerate for an hour. Place mixture in a timbale mold and shape to serve. Remove from mold onto plates and serve.

AVALON
Chef Nathan Carlson

Avocado Hummus with Toasted Pita and Tomato

I love hummus but didn't want to use only garbanzo beans and tahini, so I replaced the garbanzos with avocados. If you're having a dinner party, you can make a big bowl very easily and your guests may nosh while you finish the meal.

Serves 6 - 8

6 ripe avocados, peeled
2 cloves garlic
Juice of 2 lemons
1/2 cup tahini (sesame paste)
1/4 cup olive oil plus a few tablespoons to drizzle on pita bread
Salt and pepper to taste
8 pieces of Greek pita flat bread (not pockets)
1 large tomato, diced
1 tablespoon fresh parsley, minced

Place avocados, garlic, lemon and tahini in a food processor and purée. Slowly add olive oil. While processor is on, season with salt and pepper.

Heat oven to 350 degrees. Cut pita bread into quarters. Place on a sheet pan and drizzle with olive oil. Place in the oven and bake until just toasted, about 8 minutes.

Toss diced tomato with parsley and a bit of pepper.

Place hummus in the center of a pretty bowl. Arrange toasted pita bread around the edges. Drizzle with olive oil and sprinkle on some chopped tomatoes and herbs.

AZALEA RESTAURANT
Chef Bob Borgerding

Tuna Tartare Napoleon with
Avocado, Yellow Tomato and Crabmeat

Serves 8

1 pound sushi grade tuna, blood line removed
1 pound pasteurized crabmeat
3 ripe avocados
2 ripe yellow tomatoes, diced into 3/8" cubes
1/2 half red onion, minced
1 red tomato, seeded and diced
Salt and pepper to taste

Cut the tuna into 3/8" cubes. Refrigerate until needed.

Cut the avocados in half and remove the pit, but do not throw away the pit. Remove the flesh of the avocado from the skin and cut into a medium dice and place in a bowl with the pit of the avocado. (Keeping the pit near the flesh prevents the flesh from turning brown). Add the red onion and red tomato. Mix gently. Add salt and pepper. Place in the refrigerator until needed.

Run your fingers through the crabmeat, removing any pieces of shells.

Assembly for each serving: On a chilled plate and using a 2" wide and 2" to 3" tall ring mold, place the diced yellow tomatoes in the mold. Tamp down onto the plate. Then add the tuna and tamp again. Add the avocado relish and tamp again. Finish with the crabmeat. Remove the mold. Repeat with other portions. Serve.

Brie Salad

Serves 4

12 ounces field mix
3/4 cup dried cranberries
3/4 cup pistachios
1 cup mandarin oranges
8 ounces brie
4 ounces raspberry vinaigrette

Raspberry Vinaigrette
1/4 cup raspberry vinegar
1/2 cup canola olive oil blend

Toss field greens with the vinaigrette to your personal preference. Divide greens onto four plates. Distribute cranberries and mandarin oranges evenly over the greens. Add pistachios.

Cut brie into four even portions. Put on microwave safe plate and place in microwave on High for about 2 minutes until brie is soft and melted. Place carefully with a knife or fork on salad. Serve.

Raspberry Vinaigrette
Place vinegar in a food processor or stainless steel bowl. Slowly add oil until it reaches the desired consistency.

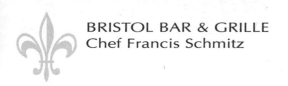
BRISTOL BAR & GRILLE
Chef Francis Schmitz

Artichoke Fritters

Chef Francis Schmitz: "These artichoke fritters are not a Bristol Bar & Grille original menu item, but they are close to it. Doug Gossman and Tim Martin, two of the original owners, discovered this appetizer while on a trip to Chicago. Doug described the dish to Lon Durbin, the Bristol Bar & Grille's chef, and Lon came up with this recipe. The rest is history."

Serves 4 to 5

Four 13.75 ounce cans of artichoke quarters,
drained and roughly chopped
3 large eggs, slightly whipped
3 tablespoons Dijon mustard
2 1/2 teaspoons red wine vinegar
1 cup flour
Dash of Cavendars or salt and pepper to taste
Canola oil for deep frying

Rémoulade Sauce
6 ribs celery, cleaned and roughly chopped
1/2 bunch parsley, washed and trimmed
1/2 cup Dijon mustard
1 small onion, peeled and roughly chopped
3/4 cup olive oil
2 tablespoons red wine vinegar
2 1/2 teaspoons dried basil
2 tablespoons paprika

In a bowl, combine eggs, mustard, vinegar, flour and Cavendars or salt and pepper. Fold in artichokes.

Fill deep fryer with oil according to manufacturer's directions. Preheat to 350 degrees. Spoon fritter batter into hot grease and fry until golden brown, approximately 3 to 5 minutes for each batch of fritters.

Serve with Rémoulade Sauce.

Rémoulade Sauce
Place all ingredients in the bowl of a food processor and purée well.

Smoked Salmon with
Burgundy Onions and Dill Mayonnaise

Serves 2

4 slices white bread, crusts removed and toasted
8 slices Nova smoked salmon
4 teaspoons capers

Burgundy Onions
1 large red onion, sliced
1 cup light brown sugar
1/2 cup raspberry vinegar

Dill Mayonnaise
1/2 cup mayonnaise
1 tablespoon lemon juice
2 tablespoons fresh dill, chopped

Burgundy Onions
In a small sauce pan, add onions, sugar and vinegar. Cook on medium high for 15 minutes. Remove from heat and cool.

Dill Mayonnaise
Mix all ingredients well and chill.

To serve: Cut toast into triangles and place on two plates. Place salmon on each toast point. Top salmon with onions. Add capers. Serve with dill mayonnaise on the side.

CAFÉ METRO
Chef Michael Crouch

Tempura Fried Prawns with Blue Cornmeal and Cilantro Lime Aioli

Serves 6

2-1/2 cups all purpose flour
1 cup blue cornmeal
(Plain cornmeal works just as well)
Salt and pepper
1 to 2 cups ice cold soda water
12 prawns or large shrimp
Peanut oil for frying
Greens of your choice

Cilantro Lime Aioli
2 egg yolks
1 tablespoon garlic, minced
Juice of two limes
2 tablespoons cilantro, chopped
Approximately 3 cups olive oil
Salt and freshly ground pepper
1 teaspoon white vinegar

In a medium bowl, mix flour and cornmeal with a bit of salt and pepper. Add ice cold soda water and stir with a wooden spoon or a handle of a utensil so that the batter remains somewhat lumpy and the consistency of paste (it should cling to the prawns). Dip a prawn into the batter and fry in a deep fryer at 400 degrees until golden brown on both sides. (If you do not have a deep fryer, you can use a pan with 2 to 3 inches of oil in it. But, make sure you keep it at 400 degrees). Remove prawns from the oil and drain on a paper towel. Serve on a bed of greens. Drizzle with aioli. Serve immediately.

Cilantro Lime Aioli
In a medium bowl, whisk eggs very slowly. Add olive oil and continue to whisk rapidly so you do not break the sauce. When about half of the oil has been added, you may add the oil a bit faster. Once all the oil is blended in, add the garlic, lime juice, salt and pepper. Finally, add the vinegar and mix well.

Bacon Wrapped Scallops with Corn Fritters and Beurre Blanc

Serves 8

24 pieces 10-20 count chemical free sea scallops
24 slices applewood smoked bacon
Olive oil (for brushing tops of scallops)
Kosher salt and freshly ground pepper, to taste
Corn Fritters (see below)
Beurre Blanc (see below)

Corn Fritters
2 cups frozen corn
1/2 tablespoon baking powder
1-1/4 cups all purpose flour
1/2 cup scallions, chopped
1 egg
1/2 cup water
1 tablespoon kosher salt
Canola oil to coat bottom of fry pan

Beurre Blanc
1 cup white wine
1 shallot, minced
Juice of one lemon
1 sprig of fresh thyme
1 bay leaf
6 black peppercorns
Pinch kosher salt
1 cup heavy cream
1/4 pound unsalted butter, softened and cubed

Remove adductor muscles from the side of each scallop. Trim each slice of bacon so it is long enough to wrap around the scallops, about one and a half times, and a little less wide than the scallops are tall. Wrap each scallop in a slice of bacon and secure with a toothpick. Brush the top and bottom of each scallop with olive oil. Season the scallops with salt and pepper. Arrange the scallops on a sheet pan and place in a 500 degree oven. Roast until the scallops are firm and the bacon is done, but not crispy. Remove the toothpicks from the scallops and place each scallop atop a warm corn fritter. Drizzle with a bit of the beurre blanc and serve immediately.

Corn Fritters
While the corn is still frozen, place 1 cup of the corn in a mixing bowl and the other cup in a food processor. Grind the frozen corn in the food processor for about a minute until you have a coarse powder. Add the ground corn to the mixing bowl along with the baking powder, flour, scallions, egg, water and salt. Mix well.

Allow the batter to sit for about 1/2 hour. Stir briefly. To cook the corn fritters, place canola oil in a heavy skillet over medium heat. When the oil is hot, but not smoking, carefully drop rounded teaspoons full of the batter into the pan. After about 1 minute, turn the fritters and cook on the second side until done.

Beurre Blanc
In a small heavy bottom saucepan, combine all ingredients except cream and butter. Bring to a boil. Lower heat to medium high and reduce until there is about 1/2 cup of liquid left. Add the cream and return to the heat. Reduce again until there is about 1/2 cup of liquid left. Remove from heat and strain into a clean pan to remove the solids. With the pan off the heat, gradually whisk in the softened butter bit by bit. Serve immediately.

Serving suggestion: I like to serve the scallops with a salad of microgreens – preferably arugula and beet sprouts, dressed simply with a little lemon juice and olive oil They pair well with a nice buttery Chardonnay.

Avocado and Goat Cheese Quesadilla with Green Onion

Serves 1

Two 6" flour tortillas
1 ripe avocado, scooped out of its skin and mashed
2 ounces mild cheddar cheese, shredded
1 ounce plain soft goat cheese
1 teaspoon green onion, chopped; save a pinch for garnish
2 tablespoons corn oil

Sprinkle cheddar cheese, goat cheese, green onion and avocado on one tortilla. Cover it with the other tortilla and push down lightly. Heat oil in a sauté pan until the oil smokes. Lay the quesadilla in the pan and turn the heat down to medium. Check the under side of the quesadilla for doneness. When it is nice and brown, flip the quesadilla and cook the other side. Remove from the pan and cut the quesadilla into 6 triangles. Arrange on a plate with triangle tips facing out. Sprinkle with remaining green onion.

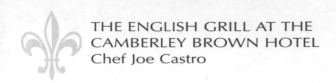

Steamer Clams with Country Ham, Garlic, Tomatoes and Parsley

Serves 4

2 tablespoons unsalted butter
16 clams, cleaned and brushed
6 ounces country ham
3 tablespoons garlic, chopped
1/2 cup Roma tomatoes, diced
3 tablespoons Italian parsley, chopped
1 bay leaf
1 teaspoon black pepper
Salt and pepper to taste
2 tablespoons olive oil
Crusty bread

Using a pot that will handle 16 clams and that has a lid, heat the butter to medium heat. Once it is hot, add 1 tablespoon of garlic, then the clams. Move them around for one minute, being careful not to burn the garlic. Add the chicken stock, bay leaf and 1 teaspoon of black pepper. Cover and cook until clams pop open and are cooked.

Put olive oil in a sauté pan over medium heat. Add 2 tablespoons of garlic followed by the country ham. Cook for 3 minutes. Add the tomatoes and parsley. Sprinkle over cooked clams.

Presentation: Serve the clams in the pot you cooked them in, topped with the country ham. Break and tear the crusty bread and garnish around the pot in a rustic manner. It's all about the clams and dipping bread.

**EQUUS RESTAURANT/
JACK'S LOUNGE**
Chef Dean Corbett

Equus Shrimp Jenkins

This dish was inspired by working with Chef Mark Jenkins, of the Bourbon Orleans, in New Orleans, and Chef Mark Stevens, of Stevens and Stevens, of Louisville.

I like to use rock shrimp for this dish because of their sweet, succulent flavor. However, any peeled and deveined shrimp will do.

4 small servings

1 pound rock shrimp, peeled and deveined
4 ounces cold butter
4 ounces brown sugar
1 teaspoon shallots minced
1/2 teaspoon garlic, minced
1 teaspoon fresh rosemary, chopped
Juice from 1 lemon
2 ounces white wine
5 ounces Worcestershire Sauce
1 teaspoon Tabasco
1 to 2 ounces bourbon (preferably Old Forester!), depending on strength desired
2 ounces cold butter, to finish

Sauce

In a hot sauté pan, melt 2 ounces of cold butter. Quickly add brown sugar, garlic, shallots, and rosemary. Caramelize on high heat until shallots become translucent. Deglaze with lemon juice and white wine. Reduce volume by one-third. Add Worcestershire, Tabasco, bourbon and shrimp to pan. Reduce heat to simmer. Turn shrimp so that they cook on both sides. Finish dish with remainder of cold butter. Chopped parsley, diced peppers or diced tomatoes may be added for garnish or color.

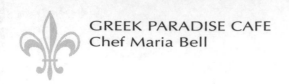
Pandaisia

Serves 10 - 14

1-1/2 pounds salmon (see below)
1 teaspoon salt
1 cup crabmeat
1 cup salad shrimp, already shelled and deveined
2 tablespoons garlic, chopped
1 tablespoon extra virgin olive oil
1 cup mayonnaise

To prepare salmon: Cover salmon with water. Add one teaspoon salt. Boil about 5 minutes or until salmon loses its reddish color. Drain and cool.

Place all ingredients in a food processor and blend well. Serve with pita bread or crackers.

JACK FRY'S RESTAURANT
Chef Shawn Ward

Diver Scallops with Kentucky Bibb Lettuce and Black Truffle Oil

Serves 4

8 diver scallops
2 tablespoons peanut oil
6 ounces pepper infused chicken stock (see recipe)
2 tablespoons lettuce purée (see recipe)
Drop of black truffle oil
(available in gourmet specialty shops)
2 teaspoons brown butter (see recipe)

Pepper Infused Chicken Stock
1 quart chicken stock
(or canned low sodium chicken broth)
4 whole black peppercorns
2 whole white peppercorns

Lettuce Purée
4 heads Kentucky Bibb lettuce,
rinsed and stems removed
2 quarts chicken stock
(or canned low sodium chicken broth)

Brown Butter
1 shallot, minced
1 teaspoon Dijon mustard
Juice of one lemon
1 teaspoon aged balsamic vinegar
1/4 cup olive oil
8 ounces unsalted butter

Sear 8 fresh diver scallops in 2 tablespoons of oil for two minutes per side. Remove from pan and reserve on heated plate. Deglaze pan with 6 ounces of pepper infused chicken stock and bring to a boil. Add 2 tablespoons of lettuce purée, a drop of black truffle oil and two teaspoons of brown butter. Whisk continuously and pour over scallops.

Pepper Infused Chicken Stock
Simmer all ingredients over low heat for 30 minutes.

Lettuce Purée
Simmer chicken stock and blanch lettuce for 20 - 30 seconds or until limp. Drain and cool in ice water. Purée in blender and strain.

Brown Butter
Place butter in saucepan over low heat. Simmer until light brown or scent is that of toasted hazelnuts. Strain and cool.

In blender, blend remaining ingredients with brown butter. Refrigerate.

Presentation: Place two seared scallops in center of hot bowl and spoon sauce around.

Shrimp Ceviche

Serves 8

Kosher salt, to taste
2 pounds medium-small shrimp, peeled and deveined
Juice from 8 limes
Juice from 8 lemons
Juice from 2 oranges, preferably sour oranges
2 large tomatoes, cut into 1/2-inch dice
1 red onion, cut into 1/2-inch dice
1 bunch cilantro, stemmed and roughly chopped
1 serrano chile, roughly chopped
2 large avocados, peeled, seeded, and cut into 1/2-inch dice
1 large cucumber, peeled and cut into 1/2-inch dice
Tortilla chips, for garnish

In a large pot of boiling salted water, add the shrimp and simmer until just cooked through, about 5 minutes. Using a slotted spoon, transfer the shrimp to a bowl of ice water to chill.

Drain the shrimp, cut into 1" pieces, and transfer to a bowl. Add the lime, lemon, and orange juice. Stir to combine, and refrigerate for at least 4 hours and up to 6 hours.

Stir the tomato, onion, cilantro, and chile into the shrimp mixture and let sit at room temperature for about 20 minutes.

When ready to serve, gently stir in the avocado and cucumber. Divide the ceviche among eight chilled martini glasses and tuck two or three tortilla chips around the sides of each.

Dungeness Crabcakes with Butternut Squash Puree and Citrus Beurre Blanc

Serves 4 - 6

1/4 cup mayonnaise
1 egg
2 tablespoons chives, chopped
2 tablespoons parsley, chopped
Hot sauce to taste
1 teaspoon garlic, chopped
1 teaspoon basil, chopped
1 teaspoon thyme, chopped
Juice of one lemon
1 teaspoon Worcestershire
1/4 cup breadcrumbs
1 pound Dungeness crabmeat

Butternut Squash Puree
1 medium butternut squash
1/4 cup butter
1 tablespoon brown sugar
salt to taste

Citrus Beurre Blanc
1/2 cup orange juice
1 tablespoon shallots, chopped
1 teaspoon butter
1 cup heavy cream
1 pound whole butter
Salt and pepper to taste

Mix together all ingredients. Fold in crabmeat. Form into patties about 4 ounces each. Coat with breadcrumbs. Sauté in clarified butter. Drain. Garnish with Butternut Squash Purée and Citrus Beurre Blanc.

Butternut Squash Purée

Cut squash in half. Place down on sheet pan. Bakc for 30 - 40 minutes at 350 degrees. Remove meat from squash and place in a mixing bowl. Whip in butter, salt and brown sugar.

Citrus Beurre Blanc

Sauté shallots in butter. Add orange juice. Reduce by half. Add cream. Reduce by half. Whisk in butter and salt and pepper.

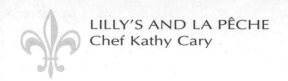

Crab Garlic Custard on Organic Spinach with Warm Bacon Dressing

Serves 8 - 12

Crab Garlic Custard	Bacon Dressing
1 cup Dungeness crabmeat	*6 slices bacon*
9 garlic cloves, peeled	*1 cup apple cider vinegar*
1 tablespoon olive oil	*1/3 cup brown sugar*
2 egg yolks	*1 teaspoon dry mustard*
2 eggs	*2 teaspoons celery seed*
1 cup heavy cream	*Kosher salt*
Cayenne pepper to taste	*Pepper*
Kosher salt	*1/3 cup olive oil*

1 pound organic spinach, washed
Toasted pine nuts (optional)

Crab Garlic Custard

Sauté whole peeled garlic cloves in olive oil until brown. Remove with a slotted spoon from pan and purée in a food processor. When well blended, add eggs and yolks, slowly adding cream. Add crab, salt and cayenne. Spoon into oiled 2" muffin tins. Place muffin tins in a large pan filled half way with water. Bake at 350 degrees for 35 minutes. Gently remove custards from muffin tins and keep warm.

Bacon Dressing

Cook bacon, chop and set aside, reserving bacon grease. In a sauce pan, cook brown sugar with vinegar until reduced by half. Whisk in dry mustard, celery seed, salt, pepper, olive oil and reserved bacon grease.

To assemble: Place spinach on plates. Top with crab garlic custard and drizzle with bacon dressing. Garnish with toasted pine nuts (optional).

Black Bean Chili

Serves 8

1/4 cup olive oil
1/2 yellow onion, small dice
1/2 green bell pepper, small dice
1 fresh jalapeño, seeded and minced
1 teaspoon garlic, minced
1/2 teaspoon cayenne pepper
1-1/2 tablespoon chili powder
2 teaspoons salt
4 pounds canned black beans
11 ounces canned crushed tomatoes
3 ounces canned diced green chiles
1 teaspoon cumin

Place olive oil in heavy bottom pot over medium heat. Add onions, green bell pepper, jalapeño pepper and garlic. Sauté until onions are beginning to soften, about 5 minutes. Make sure the vegetables are tender at this point since they will not cook that much longer when other ingredients are added. Add all remaining ingredients. Stir well to combine. Bring to a simmer and cook for about 15 minutes. Taste for seasonings, especially salt. Adjust if necessary.

Granchio Torcello
(Crab Cakes)

Serves 4 to 6

1 pound blue lump crabmeat (picked over)
1/2 cup green bell peppers, diced
1/2 cup red bell peppers, diced
1/2 cup yellow bell peppers, diced
1 tablespoon olive oil
1/4 cup red onion, diced
3 cloves garlic, diced
1 rib of celery, diced
1-1/2 cup fresh bread crumbs
3 eggs
2/3 cup mayonnaise
2 teaspoons fresh parsley, chopped
1 teaspoon Italian seasoning
1/3 cup olive oil

Rémoulade Sauce
1/2 cup mayonnaise
2 tablespoons sour cream
1 teaspoon capers, minced
1 teaspoon sour pickles, minced
1 teaspoon shallots, minced
1 teaspoon fresh chives, minced
1 teaspoon fresh parsley, minced
1 teaspoon fresh tarragon, minced
1 teaspoon Worcestershire Sauce
1/2 teaspoon freshly ground pepper
1/2 teaspoon tarragon vinegar, red wine vinegar
or white wine vinegar

Sauté green peppers, red peppers, yellow peppers, red onion, garlic and celery in 1 tablespoon of olive oil until tender.

Combine all ingredients except the remaining 1/3 cup of olive oil. Mix thoroughly and portion into 3 ounce cakes, each about 1/2" thick. Pan fry cakes in the 1/3 cup of olive oil until outsides are golden brown and crisp.

Serve with Rémoulade sauce or your favorite tartar sauce and fresh lemon.

Serves 4 to 6 people as an appetizer. Or, the crab cakes can be portioned into silver dollar size cakes and served as an hors d'oeuvre for 12 to 15 people.

Rémoulade Sauce
Mix all ingredients with a wire whisk until fully incorporated. Chill for 2 hours.

Black Bean Cakes

Serves 4

3/4 cup cooked black beans
(to cook the beans from scratch, follow the directions
on the package of dry black beans; or you may use canned beans)
1 cup Maseca corn flour
(available in specialty markets)
1/2 cup all purpose white or whole wheat flour
Salt to taste
Water

Pico de Gallo
1 tomato, chopped
1/2 large purple onion, chopped
1/2 bunch cilantro, chopped
Juice of 1 lime
Dollop of sour cream
3 cups vegetable oil
Chiles (jalapeño, serrano or habanero), if desired, and to taste
Sour cream for garnish

To prepare Pico de Gallo (salsa): Mix the tomato, onion and cilantro. Add chiles, if desired. Set aside.

Mix black beans with both flours. Add enough water to mix until the dough becomes the consistency of pizza dough. It should be a blackish grey color. Salt to taste.

Divide the dough into 10 parts and hand roll into small tortilla shaped patties. Heat oil until it is very hot. Fry the patties until they are toasty brown. Drain on paper towel.

Serve the bean cakes with salsa on top. Add sour cream to garnish.

Chicken and Green Chili Wontons with Ginger/Soy Dipping Sauce

Yield: 4 dozen

2 whole chicken breasts

Marinade for Chicken
1/4 cup soy sauce
1/2 cup sweet chili sauce
1/2 teaspoon fresh ginger

Mix ingredients and add chicken.
Cover and marinate overnight.

1 stalk celery
5 scallions, chopped
1 roasted red pepper (fresh or canned)
1 tablespoon ginger
1 cup canned diced green chilis

1 cup mixed Monterey Jack and
Cheddar cheeses, shredded
Soy sauce
Sweet chili sauce

Won ton wrappers
Oil for deep frying
Parsley to garnish

Dipping Sauce
2 cups low sodium soy sauce
1 cup sugar
1/2 cup fresh ginger, coarsely chopped
1/2 cup scallions (white part), chopped
3/4 cup hoisin sauce
1 cup cornstarch

Remove chicken from marinade and place on a baking sheet and bake at 350 degrees until done, about 20 - 25 minutes. Remove. Coarsely chop chicken, then place in a food processor and pulse until finely chopped but not puréed. Place chicken in a medium bowl. Add celery, scallions, red pepper and ginger to food processor and process as you did the chicken. Add this mixture to the chicken. Add green chilis and cheese and mix well. If mixture is too dry, add a small amount each of soy sauce and chili sauce.

Lay out a won ton wrapper on a cutting board (plastic works best). Fill only a few wrappers at a time because they dry out very quickly. Starting with one corner of the wrapper facing you (diamond shape), place a small amount of filling onto the wrapper. Roll one half way up until you have a triangle shape. Pick up the wrapper between your thumb and middle finger. Dip one end of the won ton wrapper into water. Wrap wet end of wrapper around your thumb. Fold the other side over and press.

Deep fry wontons in oil at 375 degrees for 2 to 3 minutes or until browned and floating. Remove and drain.

Dipping Sauce
Combine first five ingredients in a stock pot. Mix well to stir in sugar. Bring to a boil to melt the sugar. Reduce heat and simmer 15 minutes. Mix cornstarch with about 1/2 cup water. Use this mixture to thicken sauce, as needed. Strain and cool.

To serve: Place a small pool of sauce in a shallow bowl. Place wontons on sauce facing inward forming a circle around the edge of the bowl. Garnish with parsley or your favorite fresh herb.

SHARIAT'S
Chef Anoosh Shariat

Individual Roasted Exotic Mushroom and Root Vegetable Tartlets

6 servings

*1/2 pound shitake mushrooms,
cleaned and stemmed
1/2 pound crimini mushrooms,
cleaned and stemmed
1/2 pound portobello mushroom,
cleaned and stemmed
1 head garlic, cut in half
1 bunch fresh thyme
1-1/2 cups vegetable stock, or water
6 baby carrots, peeled and halved*

*6 baby rutabagas, peeled and halved
1/2 bulb fennel, cut into batonnets (small sticks)
1 celery root, peeled and cut into 1/4" slices
Salt and white pepper to taste
6 cups unbleached flour
2-1/4 cups unsalted butter
1 tablespoon kosher salt
1 cup ice water
Egg wash*

Cut any very large mushrooms into pieces of about 1 to 1-1/2 inches. Place the mushrooms in a small roasting pan with the garlic, thyme and stock. Cover with foil and roast at 400 degrees for 10 minutes. Remove from the oven and strain, reserving the liquid. Cover and continue to roast for an additional 10 minutes. Gently squeeze the mushrooms and garlic, adding the resulting juice to the reserved liquid. Cool the mushrooms and discard the garlic.

Blanch the carrots, rutabaga, fennel and celery root in salt water until half cooked. Shock them in an ice bath, and drain thoroughly. Reduce the reserved mushroom juice to about 3 concentrated tablespoons and toss with the mushrooms and the vegetable mixture. Lightly season to taste with salt and pepper.

To prepare the dough: Cut butter roughly into 1/2" pieces. Refrigerate. Sift the flour and salt into a large mixing bowl. With your hands, quickly work the butter into the flour until the mixture forms small

balls. Using only as much as needed to make the dough come together, work cold water into the dough. Do not overmix; the dough should still have visible pieces of butter. Let the dough rest for 1/2 hour.

Butter and flour eight 4" to 5" tart pans with removable bottoms. Roll half the dough out to a thickness of 1/16." Cut eight circles 7" in diameter, and line the pans with the dough. Adjust the seasoning in the filling, if necessary. Spoon in the filling, packing the pans full. Roll out remaining dough. Cut out 8 slightly smaller circles, and cover the mushrooms with the pastry. Seal the edges closed. Refrigerate for an hour or two.

Brushing the pastry with a simple egg wash will create a glazed effect when the pastry is baked, but it is optional. Cut a small vent into the top of each tartlet. Bake at 400 degrees for 30 minutes or until golden.

Salmon Spread

(Smoked or fresh salmon)

In the restaurant, I use salmon that has been smoked in-house over hickory. However, this step is optional. If you wish to start with smoked salmon from the grocery store, that's fine, but choose one that has been "hot smoked" or is fully cooked. If you choose not to use smoked salmon, start with fresh salmon, then remove the skin and cook using any suitable method. Poaching, steaming, baking, grilling or pan searing willall work great and will each impart its own unique flavor to this dish.

Serves 6 to 8

1 pound salmon, fully cooked or cooled (see above)
2 tablespoons mayonnaise
2 teaspoons Dijon mustard
1/3 cup red onion, diced small
1/3 cup fennel bulb, diced small
1/3 cup capers (rinsed with cold water)
1/4 cup fresh basil, chopped
1/4 cup scallions, chopped
1 pinch salt
1 teaspoon freshly ground black pepper
Crackers or thin garlic toast

Combine all ingredients in a mixing bowl and smash together with a wooden spoon, leaving some small lumps of salmon.

Serve in the center of a platter and surround with toast points. Sprinkle with chopped fennel leaves for garnish.

THE FLAGSHIP AT THE
GALT HOUSE HOTEL AND SUITES
Chef Tim W. Baker

Tomato Bisque with White Bean Relish and Parmigiano-Reggiano

Serves 4

1/4 cup olive oil
1 cup yellow onion, diced
1/2 cup carrots, diced
1/2 cup celery, diced
4 cloves garlic, roughly chopped
3 tablespoons fresh thyme, chopped
3 tablespoons fresh oregano, chopped
5 leaves fresh basil
Two 28-ounce cans whole peeled tomatoes
2 ounces stale French bread, torn into small pieces
5 cups chicken stock
1 pint heavy cream
Kosher salt and freshly ground black pepper to taste

White Bean Relish
3 cups white beans, cooked and drained
(may use canned beans, drained)
1/4 cup red onion, finely diced
1/4 cup fennel bulb, finely diced
1/4 cup roasted red pepper, finely diced
1/4 cup escarole, frisée or endive, julienned
2 tablespoons Italian parsley, julienned
2 tablespoons fresh basil, julienned
3/4 cups extra virgin olive oil
1 tablespoons black truffle oil (optional)
Kosher salt and freshly ground black pepper to taste

Parmigiano-Reggiano to garnish

Heat a large, heavy bottom saucepan on medium heat. Add olive oil, onions, celery, carrots and garlic. Cook until soft and lightly browned. Add fresh herbs, tomatoes, bread and chicken stock. Bring to a boil and simmer until soup starts to thicken (about 30 minutes). Remove from heat and allow to cool Place into blender and purée. Return to sauce pan on medium heat. Stir in heavy cream and simmer. Season with kosher salt and pepper.

White Bean Relish
Combine above ingredients. Season with salt and pepper.

Presentation: Ladle tomato bisque into bowls. Garnish with white bean relish and shaved Parmigiano-Reggiano.

Peppered Wild Mushroom Cappuccino

Serves 8

2 pounds wild mushrooms (preferably porcini), sliced
3 shallots, sliced
2 cloves garlic, mashed
2 tablespoons olive oil
2 cups white wine
2 cups vegetable broth
3 sprigs fresh thyme
1 sprig fresh rosemary
Course sea salt, to taste
White peppercorns, coarsely ground, to taste
2 cups evaporated skim milk, whipped until frothy
Fresh nutmeg, grated, for garnish

Place the oil in a heavy bottom pot over a medium heat. Add the shallots and garlic and sweat for 5 minutes. Stir well and add the herbs. Sauté for another 3 to 4 minutes. Increase the heat and add the mushrooms. Sauté mushrooms 4 to 5 minutes. Then, deglaze the pan with white wine and bring to a simmer. Once the mixture comes to a simmer, add the vegetable broth and return it to a medium heat. Reduce the mixture by one quarter and purée the soup using a blender. Season with salt and pepper. Pour the soup into coffee cups. Serve with frothed milk and top with freshly grated nutmeg.

**THE PALMER ROOM AT
LAKE FOREST COUNTRY CLUB**
Chef Annette Saco

Seared Sea Bass with Hazelnut Vinaigrette with Exotic Field Greens

Serves 1

1-1/2 cup field greens
4 ounces sea bass (Chilean)
1/4 cup sherry vinegar
1/4 cup hazelnut oil
1/4 cup walnut oil
1 shallot, minced
2 red mini plum tomatoes
2 yellow mini plum tomatoes
Salt and pepper

To prepare the vinaigrette: In a mixing bowl, add sherry and shallots, then slowly drizzle hazelnut and walnut oils and whisk together. Salt and pepper to taste.

Pour vinaigrette on field greens and place in the middle of a plate.

Heat a skillet and add 1 tablespoon of oil, salt, pepper and sea bass. Sear sea bass about 4 minutes on both sides. Preheat oven to 350 degrees and finish sea bass in the oven.

Place fish on a plate in front of the field greens and place one red and one yellow tomato on each side. Drizzle fish and plate with sherry vinaigrette.

Roasted Yellow Beet Salad with Cranberry Vinaigrette

Serves 4

1 pound yellow beets
1/2 cup olive oil
Sprig of rosemary
1/4 teaspoon Dijon mustard
6 tablespoons apple cider vinegar
1/4 cup puréed cranberries
2 tablespoons honey
1/4 cup grapeseed oil
1/2 cup canola oil
Kosher salt
Cracked black pepper
1/2 cup toasted walnuts
1/2 cup red onion, julienned
1/4 cup buttermilk Blue cheese
3 or 4 slices apple smoked bacon, fried

Remove greens from beets and wash. Place beets in a bowl and coat with olive oil, salt, pepper and rosemary. Place in a pan and cover. Roast in a 350 degree oven until fork tender, approximately 30 - 35 minutes. Let the beets cool, then peel and slice them. Place the beet slices on a plate or mix with remaining ingredients. Toss dressing lightly with greens, walnuts, red onion, buttermilk blue cheese and apple smoked bacon.

Seared Foie Gras with a Pear Semillon Coulis and Aged Balsamic

Serves 4

10 ounces Grade A foie gras
3 ripe pears, preferably Comice
2 tablespoons butter
3/4 cup Semillon wine
Kosher salt
Ground black pepper
4 tablespoons aged balsamic vinegar, at least 6 years old

To prepare the coulis: Peel and core the pears. Put one aside, quarter and slice the other two. In a small non-reactive saucepan on medium heat, add the butter, then the sliced pears. After 2 to 3 minutes, add the wine and turn the heat down to a simmer. After about 15 minutes of cooking, add the pinch of salt. Blend the mixture and set aside.

The next step is to portion the foie gras. I find it easier to slice with a hot knife. You can use hot water to do so. I figure four even 2-1/2 ounce pieces. Once the foie gras is portioned, lightly score one side of each piece for presentation. Season the scored side liberally with salt and pepper. Heat up a preferably heavy sauté pan to a medium high heat, then add the foie gras to the dry pan, scored side down first. Once it is a nice dark brown color, flip each piece over. The whole process of cooking the foie gras should not take more than 2 to 3 minutes. Ideally, just the very center of each piece should be cold, while most of it is warm. At this point, set it on a cooling rack.

For presentation: Spoon about two tablespoons of coulis in the center of each plate. Then, slice the remaining pear and put three slices in the coulis and set the foie gras next to the pear slices. For the final touch, drizzle 1 tablespoon of aged balsamic in and around the coulis, and serve immediately.

Bacon-Wrapped Sea Scallops and Portobello Mushrooms

Serves 6

1 pound 10/20 sea scallops
4 portobello mushrooms, cut into 1/2" strips
1 pound bacon, cut into strips
Freshly ground black pepper, to taste
1/2 cup soy sauce

Preheat broiler or grill. Sprinkle soy sauce and black pepper onto scallops and mushroom sticks. Wrap one scallop and one mushroom strip together with one strip of bacon. Broil until bacon is crisp. Turn periodically while broiling or grilling. Serve warm.

VINCENZO'S
Chef Agostino Gabriele

Tortino Di Melenzane Con Risotto E Funghetti Di Bosco
(Eggplant Torte filled with Risotto and Wild Mushrooms garnished with grilled shrimp in saffron sauce)

Serves 2

1 or 2 eggplants, depending on size
1 tablespoon olive oil
1/4 teaspoon garlic, minced
1/4 teaspoon fresh basil
1 cup Arborio rice
6 ounces wild mushrooms, cleaned and sliced
(morel, chanterelle and shitake)
1 tablespoon sun-dried tomatoes, chopped
1/2 cup extra virgin olive oil
5 tablespoons butter
1 tablespoon celery, finely chopped
1 tablespoon carrots, finely chopped
3 tablespoons onions, finely chopped

1 tablespoon Parmigiano
1 tablespoon parsley
1 quart chicken stock
Salt and pepper to taste
2 jumbo shrimp (optional for garnish),
peeled and deveined
1 tablespoons currants

Marinade for Shrimp
1 tablespoon olive oil
1/4 teaspoon garlic
1 teaspoon fresh basil

To prepare shrimp for garnish: Mix olive oil, garlic and basil. Add shrimp. Marinate 4 to 5 hours in refrigerator.

Slice enough eggplant into 1/8" thick slices to later be placed in individual 1 cup soufflé dishes, with eggplant slices falling over the sides of the dishes. Brush with olive oil, garlic, and basil. Place eggplant slices on a sheet pan and bake at 350 degrees for about 5 minutes or until tender. Set aside, being careful not to stack pieces on top of each other.

Melt 2 tablespoons butter in a large saucepan. Add onions, carrots, and celery. Cook for 2 minutes. Add rice and stir with wooden spoon. Gradually add 3/4 cup chicken stock and cook for 10 minutes.

In a separate skillet, sauté mushrooms and sun dried tomatoes in 1 tablespoon butter. Add cooked risotto (rice), Parmigiano and parsley. Set aside.

To prepare sauce: Sauté 2 tablespoons shallots and 1/2 teaspoon saffron in 1 tablespoon butter until shallots are brown. Add 1/4 cup chicken stock and cook until stock is reduced by half. Add 1 tablespoon butter. Salt and pepper to taste.

Remove shrimp from marinade. Broil or grill for 3 to 4 minutes.

For each serving: In a 1 cup soufflé dish coated with non stick spray, lay eggplant in crisscross fashion with the ends falling over the sides of the dish. Place risotto in the center, then fold eggplant over the rice. Place the soufflé dishes in a large pan filled with 1" water. Bake at 350 degrees for 10 minutes.

Invert tortes onto large plates for an attractive presentation. Place grilled jumbo shrimp on top. Drizzle saffron sauce over the top and sprinkle with currants for added color.

Shrimp Madagascar with Wilted Spinach

Serves 1

3 large shrimp u-10 or larger
1 tablespoon green peppercorn paste
(available in specialty markets)
1/2 teaspoon shallots, minced
1 tablespoon demi glace
1/4 cup whipping cream
1/2 ounce or more brandy
1 handful spinach
Sea salt to taste

Sauté shrimp in whole butter until opaque. Remove shrimp from pan and reserve in a warm place. Deglaze the pan with brandy, then add the other ingredients. Simmer until slightly thickened. Season with sea salt.

Garnish with tomato concassé (chopped and seeded tomato).

Entrées

Louisville's most innovative chefs have created a delectable array of entrées for you to create in your own kitchen. Some of the dishes are ideal for casual dining. Others are perfect for elegant entertaining. Whatever the occasion, remember the advice from the chefs: have patience, use your imagination and have fun cooking.

Sautéed Mahi-Mahi on Arugula with Scallop-Lobster Tortellini and Roasted Pepper Dressing

This dish was first created for *Great Chefs of the World* on the Discovery Channel.

Serves 4

Tortellini
1-1/2 cups all purpose flour
Pinch of salt
2 large eggs

Tortellini Filling
4 large scallops
2 ounces lobster meat
1 egg white
1/2 cup heavy (whipping) cream
Juice of one lemon
Salt and freshly ground pepper to taste
1 large basil leaf

Fried Eggplant Nests
4 eggplants
Canola oil for deep-frying

Dressing
1 yellow bell pepper, roasted
1 red bell pepper, roasted
2 tablespoons champagne vinegar
1/3 cup extra virgin olive oil
Salt and freshly ground pepper to taste
1 sprig cilantro, stemmed and minced

Mahi-Mahi
1/4 cup plus 1 tablespoon unsalted butter
Four 7 to 8 ounce Mahi-Mahi fillets, cut in half
(may substitute any firm white-fleshed salt water fish)
4 bunches arugula (rocket)

1 cup Beurre Blanc (recipe follows)
2 tablespoons lobster oil
(available at specialty food markets)

Beurre Blanc
Makes 1 cup

2 shallots, minced
3 tablespoons dry white wine
2 tablespoons white wine vinegar
2 tablespoons heavy (whipping) cream
Salt and freshly ground white pepper to taste
1 cup unsalted butter,
cut into tablespoon-size chunks

Beurre Blanc

Combine the shallots, wine and vinegar in a medium non-aluminum saucepan or sauté pan and cook over medium heat until the liquid is reduced to about 2 tablespoons. Whisk in the cream and reduce the heat to medium-low; cook until reduced again to about 3 tablespoons. Season with salt and pepper. Whisking rapidly, add a piece of butter. When it is nearly melted, add the next piece, continuing until all the butter has been added and the sauce is light in color and slightly thickened. If drops of liquid butter appear at any point, remove the pan from the heat and whisk in the next few bits of butter off the heat until the temperature of the sauce cools again. Use immediately or keep the sauce warm in an insulated bottle until ready to serve.

Note: The sauce may be begun as much as a day ahead and prepared to the point at which you add the seasonings; cover and refrigerate. When ready to continue, warm the reduction over medium-low heat, then proceed.

Continued on next page.

To prepare the tortellini: Combine the flour and salt and make a mound of seasoned flour on work surface. Make a crater in the top and break the eggs into the crater. With your fingers, work the eggs into the dough, gradually incorporating all the flour. Do not overwork the dough; work only until it is smooth. Form the dough into a smooth ball. Wrap the ball in plastic wrap and set aside to rest for 20 minutes.

Working with 1/3 of the dough at a time, roll through a pasta machine 4 or 5 times, following the manufacturer's directions, until the pasta is very thin and pliable. Repeat with the other sheets. With a scalloped or plain 3 1/2" cutter, cut 12 circles from the dough. Set aside for the tortellini.

To prepare the filling: Put the scallops and lobster meat in a food processor and pulse three times. Add the egg white and cream and puree; add the lemon juice while the machine is running. When smooth, check and adjust seasoning with salt and pepper. Keep the filling cold by placing the bowl containing the filling in a larger bowl of ice while using the mixture. If not using immediately, cover with plastic wrap and refrigerate until ready to use.

Lay the tortellini on a work surface. Put a generous teaspoon of filling in one of the tortellini and fold the pasta in half. Moisten the edges and press to seal, forming a scalloped margin. Fold into the traditional tortellini shape: holding a half-circle tortellini in your hands, fold in the points, overlapping them in front of the filled portion and pressing to hold them in place; they may be "tacked" with a little water if necessary. Set aside and fill all the other tortellini. Put in the refrigerator.

To prepare the eggplant: Use a mandoline or spiral slicer to cut the skin of the eggplants into very thin long strips (one eighth inch or less). Heat the oil to 370 degrees in a deep fryer or deep saucepan. Working with 1/4 of the eggplant strips

at a time, drop a tangle of strips gently into the hot oil and fry just until crisp, about 15 seconds. Remove with a slotted spoon or skimmer and drain on paper towels. Repeat until all the strips are fried and you have four clusters of fried eggplant strips.

To prepare the dressing: Peel the roasted peppers and dice the flesh into 1/4" dice. Heat the olive oil over medium heat and add the pepper dice. Cook for one minute. Stir in the champagne vinegar and season with salt, pepper and cilantro. Set aside; keep warm.

To finish the tortellini: Bring a large pot of lightly salted water to a boil, then reduce the heat to medium. Put a basil leaf in the water. Add the tortellini, a few at a time. Start the timing when they float to the surface, cooking them for 2-1/2 minutes from that time. Remove with a slotted spoon or skimmer and drain on a towel. Keep warm.

To cook the fish: Heat a medium sauté pan over medium high heat. Add 2 tablespoons of butter and cook until the solids at the bottom of the pan just begin to turn brown. Add 4 pieces of fish. Sear quickly on one side, about 30 seconds, then turn and sauté on the other side, 30 seconds to one minute, depending on the thickness of the fillets. Keep the fillets separated in the pan as they sear. Remove with a spatula and drain on paper towels. Repeat with the remaining fish.

Place the arugula in the pan and reduce the heat to medium; add the remaining tablespoon of butter and toss until the arugula wilts.

To serve: Divide the wilted arugula among the serving plates. Place 2 pieces of fish on each, one slightly overlapping the other, atop the arugula. Position 3 tortellini in the 12 o'clock, 4 o'clock and 8 o'clock positions on each plate. Spoon beurre blanc around the arugula on the plate. Drizzle with lobster oil (optional). Top each with a fried eggplant cluster.

ASIATIQUE
Chef Peng S. Looi

Grilled Curry Glazed Wahoo, Sautéed Baby Bok Choy and Mango + Strawberry Chutney

Serves 4

Fish
8 pieces of 4 ounce fresh wahoo, cut into flat fillet squares
1 tablespoon madras curry powder
2 ounces Asiatique Stir Fry Sauce
1/2 cup Chinese rice wine
1 teaspoon sesame oil
1 tablespoon virgin olive oil

Vegetables
2 tablespoons vegetable oil
2 cups baby bok choy, diced
4 shallots, sliced
Dash ginger, minced
Salt and pepper

Chutney
1 ripe mango, diced
15 fresh strawberries, diced
1 tablespoon basil, minced
4 tablespoons Thai sweet chili sauce
1 tablespoon Asiatique Stir Fry Sauce
Juice of 1/2 lime

Garnish
Fresh microgreens or small leaf herbs,
such as spicy basil or thyme

Fish
Mix curry powder, Asiatique Stir Fry sauce, rice wine, sesame oil and olive oil in a non-reactive bowl. Then, place fish in bowl to marinate thoroughly. Refrigerate for 2 hours.

Chutney
Mix all ingredients in a non-reactive bowl. Refrigerate.

Vegetables
Quickly sauté baby bok choy, shallots, ginger, and salt and pepper. Remove from pan and set aside.

Procedure: In a hot skillet with 2 teaspoons of olive oil, place 2 pieces of marinated fish. Sear for about 3 minutes on each side until fully cooked. Remove fish onto a plate and set aside. Repeat for all fillets.

In same skillet, add ginger and shallots. When translucent, add baby bok choy and sauté. Add salt and pepper to taste.

For each serving, place 1/2 cup of sautéed baby bok choy in the center of a plate. Place 1 piece of wahoo and 1 tablespoon of chutney mixture on top of bok choy. Repeat procedure. Top "tian" with micro greens or fresh herbs. Serve immediately.

Braised Baby Bok Choy with Shitake Mushrooms and Fresh Garlic

Serves 4

Sauce
1 tablespoon cornstarch
1 teaspoon sesame oil
1 tablespoon oyster sauce
1 tablespoon olive oil
2 cups fresh shitake mushrooms
1 teaspoon garlic, minced
1 teaspoon ginger root, minced
8 baby bok choy, cut lengthwise into quarters
Salt and pepper to taste

To make sauce: In a small bowl, mix cornstarch, sesame oil and oyster sauce. Set aside.

In a wok or deep skillet, heat oil over medium heat for about 30 seconds. Add mushrooms, garlic and gingerroot. Sauté until mushrooms are semi soft, about 3 to 4 minute. Add bok choy. Toss and cook briefly. Add 3 tablespoons water and bring to a boil. Turn heat to low. Cover and allow mixture to braise for 2 to 3 minutes or until vegetables are tender.

Stir in sauce ingredients and cook until slightly thickened. Season to taste with salt and pepper. Transfer to plates and serve warm.

AUGUST MOON
CHINESE BISTRO
Chef Peng S. Looi

General's Chicken

Serves 4

1 pound chicken breasts, cut into small cubes
1 egg, lightly beaten
3 tablespoons corn starch
Water for mixing
2 cups vegetable oil
1/4 bottle Asiatique Stir-Fry Sauce
2 tablespoons sugar
1 tablespoon vinegar
Tabasco or other hot sauce to taste

In a medium bowl, mix egg and chicken cubes. Add water and cornstarch until chicken is well coated. Mix well.

Place the vegetable oil in a deep fry pan. When oil is very hot, add a portion of the chicken, but do not crowd the pieces. Fry until golden brown. Remove and drain on a paper towel. Repeat in small batches until all of the chicken is browned.

In a hot sauté pan, add Asiatique Stir-Fry sauce. When sauce simmers, add sugar, vinegar and hot sauce to taste. Simmer sauce for another 30 seconds. Place chicken pieces in sauce and toss for 2 minutes. Remove and serve immediately.

AVALON
Chef Nathan Carlson

Beer and Chile Braised Boneless Short Ribs

I wanted to have some sort of rib on the Avalon menu, but I didn't want it to be too messy. I decided on boneless short ribs. Because I wanted them to be very bold and flavorful, I thought about braising them with beer and a variety of chiles. I tried it and the result was great.

Serves 4

3 pounds boneless short ribs
2 bottles dark beer, such as a Porter
1 ancho chile, roughly chopped
1 serrano chile, roughly chopped
1 poblano pepper, roughly chopped
1 yellow onion, sliced
3 cloves garlic, crushed

2 tablespoons paprika
1 stalk celery, roughly chopped
1 tomato, roughly chopped
2 tablespoons freshly ground pepper
1 tablespoon salt
2 tablespoons all purpose flour
3 tablespoons vegetable oil for searing ribs

Place a large frying pan over medium high heat and add oil. Season ribs with salt and pepper. Place all ribs in pan. Brown ribs evenly and remove from pan. In same pan, sauté chiles, onion, garlic, celery and tomato. When they start to brown, add the flour and stir all ingredients together. Pour beer into pan and mix well. Place short ribs back in pan and pour in any accumulated juices. Cover with aluminum foil and place in a 300 degree oven for 2 hours. Remove and serve.

Serving suggestion: Place the short ribs on top of a mound of mashed potatoes and pour a bit of the pan jus over the top. Finally, top with onion relish and herbs of your choice.

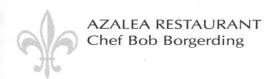

Beef Tenderloin Stuffed with Wild Mushrooms and Goat Cheese

Serves 8

Eight 8 ounce center cut filets of beef
1 pound goat cheese
1 pound wild mushrooms (shitake, crimini, porcini, morel), rinsed and dried
8 ounces cream cheese
2 tablespoons fresh herbs (basil, rosemary, thyme and oregano)
1 teaspoon garlic, minced
Salt and pepper to taste

Roughly chop the mushrooms and place in a stainless steel mixing bowl. Add the goat cheese, cream cheese, herbs and garlic. Mix until all ingredients are incorporated.

With a boning knife, hollow out a small pocket in the side of the tenderloins. With a piping bag, or with a small spoon, fill the pocket of each tenderloin with about 2 ounces of the mixture until the pocket is full.

Preheat the grill or set the broiler and grill the tenderloin approximately 3 to 4 minutes per side for rare, 8 minutes per side for medium, or approximately 12 to 14 minutes per side for well done. Serve.

The beef tenderloin may be accompanied by any starch of your choice, such as cheese grits or garlic crushed potatoes.

Tri-Colored Tortellini with Chipotle Basil Cream Sauce

Serves 4

Chipotle Basil Cream Sauce
1/4 cup olive oil
1/2 Spanish onion, diced small
1 tablespoon garlic, chopped
1/2 cup white wine
1/4 cup fresh basil, chopped
1 quart heavy cream
3/4 cup chicken consommé or bouillon
1/2 can chipotle peppers
1/2 cup cornstarch dissolved in water

Pasta
3 ounces olive oil
1 tomato, medium diced
1 cup mushrooms, sliced
4 chicken breasts,
grilled and sliced into thin strips
2 pounds tri-colored tortellini, cooked
Basil, for garnish
Parmesan cheese

Chipotle Basil Cream Sauce

In a two quart sauce pan, add olive oil. Let heat, then add diced onion and garlic. Cook until the edges of the onion begin to become translucent, then add consommé or bouillon, white wine, basil and half of the heavy cream.

In a food processor, puree the chipotle peppers and add to the sauce pan. Allow to come to a boil and slowly add the cornstarch and mix until it reaches the desired thickness.

Pasta

In a large sauté pan, add olive oil and mushrooms and allow to cook for approximately 4 minutes. Add chicken and tomatoes, stirring frequently. Add four cups of the chipotle cream sauce, thinning with heavy cream, if necessary. Add tortellini, stirring well until all ingredients are thoroughly heated. Divide onto four plates. Garnish with fresh basil and Parmesan cheese. Serve.

BRISTOL BAR & GRILLE
Chef Francis Schmitz

Pork Loin Dijonaise

Serves 4

Four 8 ounce center cut pork loins
Salt and pepper to taste

Dijonaise Sauce
1 pound butter
1 cup Dijon mustard
1 cup light brown sugar

Salt and pepper each piece of pork. Grill or broil for 12
to 15 minutes. Pour sauce over pork and serve.

Dijonaise Sauce
Melt the butter in a saucepan over low heat. Add brown
sugar and whisk until melted. Add mustard and whisk
well. Serve immediately or keep refrigerated until ready
to use. If refrigerated, warm before serving.

Trout with Almond Flour Dijonaise

Serves 2

2 tablespoons butter
2 tablespoons vegetable oil
2 pieces of 8 ounce headless trout

Candy Pecans
1/2 cup pecans, chopped
3 tablespoons caramel sundae topping

Dijon Mayonnaise
1 tablespoon smooth Dijon mustard
1/4 cup mayonnaise

Almond Flour
1-1/2 cups almonds, blanched and finely ground

1 cup all purpose flour
1/2 teaspoon salt
1/2 teaspoon white pepper

Melt 2 tablespoons butter and oil in a large sauté pan. Heat over medium heat.

Place trout, skin side down, in flour. Place the ground almonds on a plate. Flip the trout onto the almonds, meat side down. Press lightly into almonds.

Sauté trout, skin side down, in butter for 2 to 3 minutes. Carefully turn trout over and lower the heat. Sauté for 4 to 5 minutes.

Carefully remove trout and place on plates with a side of pecans and mustard.

Candy Pecans
Mix pecans and caramel topping and set aside.

Dijon Mayonnaise
Mix mustard and mayonnaise and set aside.

CAFÉ METRO
Chef Michael Crouch

Roasted Leg of Lamb Stuffed
with Wild Mushrooms and Escarole

Serves 10 - 12

2 heads of escarole, chopped
3 tablespoons butter
5 tablespoons olive oil
2 pounds wild mushrooms , sliced
(crimini, shitake, chanterelle)
1/2 cup shallots, finely chopped
2 bunches green onions, minced
3 cloves garlic, minced
1-1/2 cup bread crumbs
(from one day old French bread)

2 tablespoons whipping cream
2 tablespoons fresh thyme, chopped
1 teaspoon salt
1/2 teaspoon freshly ground black pepper
One 5-7 pound boneless leg of lamb
(Ask your butcher to butterfly the lamb for you)
1 egg, lightly beaten
4 ounces ground veal

Heat 2 tablespoons olive oil in a large skillet over medium heat. Add 2 cups escarole, the mushrooms, shallots, green onions and garlic. Sauté until tender. Add fresh thyme and salt and pepper as mixture nears becoming tender. Remove from heat and set aside. Add cream and bread crumbs.

Preheat oven to 450 degrees. Season lamb with salt and pepper. Add egg and ground veal to mushroom mixture. Mix well and stuff mixture into lamb.

Starting at the thin end, roll the lamb to hide the filling. Seal the ends with toothpicks or skewers. Tie the lamb with kitchen string every couple of inches along the entire length of the lamb. Rub the outside of lamb with oil, butter and salt and pepper.

Roast lamb on a rack in a roasting pan for approximately 1 hour and 15 minutes for medium rare (135 degrees). Remove from oven and let stand 10 minutes before carving.

Roast Breast of Chicken with Andouille-Cornbread Stuffing and Apple Cider Glaze

Serves 8

*8 large skin-on, single-lobe
free range chicken breasts
(try to find breasts with the skin completely intact, if possible)
1/4 pound butter, softened
Olive oil to coat pan and to
brush tops of chicken breasts
Kosher salt and freshly ground black pepper, to taste*

Andouille Cornbread Stuffing
*1/2 tablespoon olive oil
1/2 cup celery, finely diced
1/2 cup onion, finely diced*

*1/2 cup red bell pepper, finely diced
1 cup Andouille sausage, medium diced
1 cup Granny Smith apple, peeled and medium diced
1-1/2 cups cornbread, crumbled
(your own recipe or any good quality purchased cornbread)
1 ounce butter, melted
4 fresh sage leaves, minced
Kosher salt and freshly ground black pepper*

Apple Cider Glaze
*1 cup granulated sugar
2 cups apple cider vinegar
3 cups apple cider*

Working from the outside edge of each breast, gently separate the skin from the flesh to form a pocket. Pack a small handful of stuffing into a lump and stuff between the skin and the flesh. Gently press down on the skin to distribute the stuffing under the skin. Brush each breast with olive oil and season with salt and pepper. Arrange the breasts in a heavy roasting pan and place in a 500 degree oven. Roast until a meat thermometer inserted in the thickest part of the breast reads 150 degrees, or about 15 to 20 minutes. Remove from oven and allow to rest in a warm place for 10 minutes. Remove breasts from roasting pan to serving plates and keep warm. Place roasting pan on stovetop over medium heat. Add apple cider glaze and bring to a boil. Scrape bottom of roasting pan with a spatula to release any cooked-on juices from the chicken into the sauce. Cook for about 2 minutes. Remove from heat and whisk in softened butter. Spoon glaze over breasts and serve immediately.

Andouille Cornbread Stuffing
Heat olive oil in a large sauté pan over medium heat. Add celery, red bell pepper, onion, a heavy pinch of kosher salt and about 6 twists of freshly ground black pepper. Cook for about 2 minutes. Add Andouille sausage. Stir and continue to cook for about 4 minutes longer, until the sausage releases juices and the vegetables are cooked, but not yet soft. Add apple. Stir and return to heat for another 2 minutes. Remove from the heat and pour into a large mixing bowl. Add cornbread crumbles, sage, and butter, and mix well. A handful of the stuffing should hold its shape when squeezed. If the mixture seems a little dry add a bit more melted butter. If it seems too wet, add more cornbread crumbles. Taste and adjust salt and pepper.

Apple Cider Glaze
Combine cider, vinegar and sugar in a heavy saucepan and place over high heat. Bring to a boil. Lower heat to medium and reduce until you have about 2 cups left.

Serving suggestion: I suggest serving the stuffed chicken with simple, comforting side dishes such as smashed sweet potatoes and corn pudding.

A crisp, spicy Gewürztraminer goes well with this dish.

Red Snapper al Mojo de Ajo and Soft Tacos with Mango Salsa

Serves 4

Eight 6" flour tortillas
4 handsful salad greens or lettuce

Mojo de Ajo (slow roasted garlic):
4 tablespoons garlic, minced
3 tablespoons corn oil
Squeeze of fresh lime juice
Sea salt to taste

Red Snapper
Four 6 ounce pieces of center cut red snapper
1 cup flour
Sea salt and freshly ground pepper to taste
3 tablespoons corn oil
1 tablespoon butter

Mango Salsa
3 ripe mangos peeled and chopped
(or any tropical fruit)
1 jalapeño, minced
1 tablespoon red onion, minced
1 tablespoon red bell pepper, chopped
1 tablespoon cilantro, chopped
1/2 lime, squeezed
Pinch of sea salt

Note: You will need two 6" flour tortillas per person, a handful of salad greens or lettuce per plate, and any side dishes you like. El Mundo serves these tacos with beans and rice. Heating up the tortillas over an open flame makes them more pliable and tastier. When you are ready to cook the fish, arrange the tortillas on plates with the greens on top.

Mojo de Ajo (slow roasted garlic)

Place oil, garlic and lime juice in a sauté pan and cook on very low heat until the garlic gets soft and light brown. The low heat is important. This may take approximately 30 minutes. When ready, strain and sprinkle with sea salt. Set aside.

Mango Salsa

Mix all ingredients and set aside.

Red Snapper

Add the salt and pepper to the flour. Mix well. Place oil in a sauté pan and heat. Dredge the fish in the seasoned flour until it's covered. Shake off excess flour. When the oil smokes, lay fish in the pan and turn down the heat to medium. Don't overcrowd the pan or the fish will be soggy. Cook the fish until nice and brown, about 4 minutes. Then, flip and cook approximately 4 minutes, depending on the thickness of the fish. Remove the fish from the pan.

Arrange the fish on top of the tortillas and greens. In the same pan you cooked the fish in, add the Mojo de Ajo (garlic) and a pat of butter. Let the butter melt and warm the garlic. You do not want the garlic to get crispy. Pour the garlic butter over the fish. Place the mango salsa on the side.

Roasted Loin of Lamb with Hominy Grits

Serves 4

1 tablespoon olive oil
2 pounds loin of lamb
1/2 cup country ham
1/2 cup yellow hominy
1/4 cup mixture of red and green bell peppers, diced
1/4 cup shallots, minced

Grits
1 cup grits
2-1/2 cups chicken stock
1/4 cup green onions, sliced
1 teaspoon fresh thyme
1 tablespoon butter

Lamb

Season the lamb with salt and pepper. In a sauté pan, sear the lamb at high heat on all sides in 1 tablespoon of olive oil. Reduce heat to medium and cook to desired temperature. Remove lamb and allow to rest. Deglaze the skillet with lamb or reduced chicken stock and reduce until it coats a spoon. Whisk in 1 tablespoon of butter and season with salt and pepper.

Grits

Sauté the shallots in 1 tablespoon of butter until caramelized. Follow with the country ham, peppers and hominy. Deglaze with chicken stock and bring to a boil. Reduce to a simmer and slowly add the grits, stirring constantly until creamy. Finish with thyme and green onions. Adjust seasoning with salt and pepper.

Serve the sliced lamb nested on a portion of grits with a center garnish of the season's best vegetables. Pour the sauce over the meat.

Chipotle Rubbed Mahi-Mahi with Chorizo, Corn and Purple Potato Hash

Serves 4

4 tablespoons vegetable oil
4 tablespoons chipotle powder
2 tablespoons garlic, minced
2 tablespoons each of Dave's Herbs
(parsley, rosemary and dill), finely chopped
2 pounds Mahi-Mahi

Hash

2 pounds purple potatoes, medium dice and
cooked until tender
4 tablespoons butter
2 tablespoons garlic, minced
2 tablespoons shallots, minced
1 cup yellow corn, fresh or frozen
1/2 cup Chorizo sausage, cooked and rendered
(fat removed)
2 tablespoons each Dave's Herbs
(parsley, rosemary and dill), finely chopped
Salt and pepper, to taste

Mix the first four ingredients together. Thoroughly coat the Mahi-Mahi. Place in a covered dish and marinate in the refrigerator for at least 2 hours.

Hash

Set aside potatoes that have been drained and cooled. Sweat butter, garlic and shallots in a sauté pan until they become translucent. Add the corn, Chorizo sausage and potatoes. Fry until the mixture is thoroughly heated and browned. Season with the herbs, salt and pepper.

Presentation: Place grilled Mahi-Mahi resting on a mound of hash in the center of a plate. You may finish with guacamole and fresh tomato salsa, if desired.

Moussaka

Serves 8 - 10

3 large eggplants
2 pounds Idaho potatoes, peeled and sliced
1 onion, diced
2 pounds ground beef
1/2 cup white wine
2 tomatoes, grated
Half bunch parsley, chopped
Salt and pepper to taste
1 cup olive oil

Béchamel Sauce
4 cups warm whole milk
8 tablespoons flour
3 tablespoons unsalted butter
Salt and pepper to taste
Pinch of cinnamon or nutmeg

To prepare the Béchamel Sauce: Melt the butter in a saucepan on low heat. Add the flour and mix thoroughly. Add the milk a little at a time, stirring continuously until well blended. Add salt and pepper, and cinnamon or nutmeg. Set aside.

To prepare the Moussaka: Wrap the eggplant in aluminum foil and bake at 350 degrees until soft, approximately 20 minutes. Slice into thick slices. Put enough olive oil in a fry pan to cover the potatoes. Fry the potatoes. Drain and set aside. In another fry pan, brown the onion and ground beef together in approximately 2 tablespoons olive oil. Add tomatoes, parsley, and salt and pepper. Simmer for 15 minutes. Layer the potatoes, then the ground beef mixture, then the eggplant in a deep baking dish. Cover with the Béchamel Sauce. Bake in a 350 degree oven for 30 to 40 minutes.

Jack Fry's Pork Chop

Serves 8

Eight 12 ounce center cut rib pork chops

Rosemary Dijon Butter
1 stick unsalted butter, softened
1 tablespoon fresh rosemary
2 tablespoons Dijon mustard

Combine in a food processor and set aside.

Breading
4 cups breadcrumbs
2 tablespoons fresh rosemary
2 tablespoons fresh chives
2 tablespoons fresh parsley
1 tablespoon fresh sage

Combine in a food processor and set aside.

Topping
3 yellow onions, diced
2 tablespoons sugar
2 tablespoons olive oil
2 cups chicken stock
(or canned low sodium chicken broth)
32 garlic cloves, peeled and blanched (see below)
1-1/2 pounds shitake mushrooms, stemmed and sliced
10 medium new potatoes, peeled and quartered
16 asparagus spears, blanched and cut into 2" pieces
8 slices applewood smoked bacon

Sauce
Reserved bacon fat
1 cup dry vermouth
6 cups chicken stock
1 tablespoon fresh rosemary, chopped

To blanch and prepare the garlic: Place garlic in a colander or strainer and put strainer in a pot of boiling water for 2 to 3 minutes. Remove and place colander in ice water. Repeat process a second time. Then, place colander in boiling water for 2 to 3 minutes or until garlic is the consistency of a cooked potato. Then, place colander in ice water to stop the cooking. Remove from water and dry garlic, then sauté garlic in olive oil until golden brown. Season with salt and pepper and reserve.

To prepare the mushrooms: Sauté in olive oil and reserve.

To prepare the potatoes: Toss potatoes with olive oil. Roast until golden brown and reserve.

To prepare the bacon: Sauté until crisp. Drain on paper towels and dice. Reserve fat in pan.

Caramelize sugar in olive oil. Add onions and chicken stock and reduce by half. Add garlic cloves, mushrooms, potatoes, asparagus and bacon in a large bowl. Set aside and keep warm.

Preheat oven to 375 degrees. Brush pork chops on both sides with Dijon mustard. Season with salt and pepper. Coat pork chops with breading. Sear each chop in duck fat or reserved bacon fat on top of stove. Place on sheet pan in oven. Bake for 18 to 24 minutes. Placed each cooked pork chop on a separate plate. Ladle vegetable medley and sauce on top of each chop.

Sauce
Deglaze pan of bacon fat with vermouth. Reduce by half. Add chicken stock and rosemary and reduce by half. Add seasonings. Reserve.

Feijoada
(Brazilian Black Bean and Meat Stew)

Serves 8

For the Beans
1/4 cup olive oil
12 cups water
2 pounds dried black beans, picked over
2 large Spanish onions, chopped
4 bay leaves
1/4 cup chopped fresh garlic
2 ham hocks

For the Adobo
1/4 cup ground cumin
1/4 cup ground coriander
1/4 cup Kosher salt
2 tablespoons ground cayenne pepper
1 tablespoons adobo-style seasoning

For the Meat
2 tablespoons olive oil
1 pound breakfast sausage links
1 pound smoked sausage links
1 pound chorizo sausage
1 pound beef tenderloin, cut into 1/4-inch cubes
1 pound pork tenderloin, cut into 1/4-inch cubes

8 cups hot, cooked white rice
Pico de Gallo (see recipe)
Sautéed Greens (see recipe)
Farofa (see recipe)
Chopped scallions, for garnish
1 orange, cut into wedges

Pico de Gallo
4 large tomatoes, roughly chopped
2 serrano chiles, roughly chopped
1 medium red onion, roughly chopped
1 bunch fresh cilantro,
stemmed and roughly chopped
Juice of two lemons
Juice of two limes
Kosher salt and freshly ground black pepper, to taste

Sautéed Greens
2 pounds kale or mustard greens,
stemmed and roughly chopped
2 tablespoons olive oil
4 cloves fresh garlic, chopped
1/4 cup white wine or water
Kosher salt and freshly ground black pepper, to taste

Farofa
1 cup bacon, chopped
1/2 cup Spanish onion, chopped
1/2 cup manioc flour
(also called cassava or tapioca flour;
available at specialty food stores)
8 tablespoons unsalted butter
2 large eggs, beaten
1/4 cup scallions, chopped
Kosher salt, to taste

To prepare the beans: In a large bowl, add the beans and cover with cold water by 2 inches. Let the beans soak in the refrigerator overnight. Drain.

Heat the olive oil in a large pot over medium-high heat. Add the onions and cook, stirring, until translucent, about 8 minutes.

Meanwhile, make the adobo: In a small bowl, whisk together the cumin, coriander, salt, cayenne and adobo seasoning. Add the garlic and bay leaves to the onion and cook, stirring, until fragrant, about one minute. Add the beans, water, ham hocks and half of the adobo. Bring to a boil. Lower the heat and simmer, uncovered, stirring occasionally, until the beans are very tender, about 2 hours.

Remove the ham hocks and pull and shred the meat. Add the meat back to the stew and discard the bones. (The stew can be made up to this point up to 3 days ahead.)

To prepare the meat: In a large bowl, toss the sausages with the remaining adobo.

Heat the oil in a large cast-iron skillet over high heat. Working in batches, brown the sausages and transfer them to a plate. Roughly chop the sausages and stir them into the stew. Return the skillet to high heat and, working in batches, brown the beef and pork and add them to the stew.

Return the stew to a simmer and cook, stirring occasionally, for about 30 minutes more.

To serve: When ready to serve, arrange a mound of rice in the center of eight plates and spoon some of the stew over the top of each. Spoon some of the pico de gallo and greens on opposite sides of the stew. Sprinkle with the farofa and chopped scallions and garnish with orange wedges.

Pico de Gallo

In a large bowl, mix together all the ingredients. Let sit at room temperature for 30 minutes. Yield: about 4 cups

Sautéed Greens

Heat the oil in a large pot over medium-high heat. Add the garlic and cook, stirring, until fragrant, about 1 minute. Add the greens and wine and cook, stirring, until wilted. Lower the heat to medium and cook, stirring occasionally, until tender, about 10 minutes. Yield: 8 side-dish servings.

Farofa

Heat a large skillet over medium-high heat. Add the bacon and cook, stirring, until its fat has rendered. Add the onion and cook, stirring, until lightly browned, about 5 minutes. Add manioc flour and cook, stirring, until golden brown and toasted. Add the butter and cook, stirring, until absorbed. Add the eggs and scallion. Cook, stirring, until scrambled. Transfer the farofa to a bowl and let cool slightly. Yield: about two cups.

Churrascos De Argentina

Serves 8 - 10

Chimichurri Sauce
1 small yellow onion, quartered
1 cup red wine vinegar
Juice of 2 limes (about 2 tablespoons)
1 teaspoon salt
1/2 cup parsley leaves
1/2 cup cilantro leaves
4 cloves garlic
1 serrano chili, quartered
1 tomato, quartered
1/4 cup olive oil

Meat and Marinade
5 pounds skirt steak
(flank steak may be substituted)
3 cloves garlic, minced
2 small yellow onions, chopped
1 cup olive oil
1 tablespoon salt
1 tablespoon pepper
1 tablespoon crushed red pepper flakes
Juice of 2 limes
2 cups red wine vinegar

To make the sauce: Blend all the ingredients in a food processor or half at a time in a blender. Chill. Can be refrigerated up to 4 days. (Any sauce leftover from recipe is delicious on sandwiches).

To marinate the meat: Place meat in a large bowl for which you have a tight fitting lid, or into a large zipper style plastic bag. Add remaining ingredients, then half the chimichurri sauce (2 cups) and stir to combine.

Grill the meat about 5 minutes on each side, or until the center reaches 130 degrees. Allow meat to rest for at least 5 minutes before slicing. Cut across the grain, on an angle into 3" to 4" thick slices.

Optional pan-frying directions: Heat a large (about 12") heavy skillet over high heat until it's hot enough to sizzle drops of water. Sear steaks 4 to 5 minutes on the first side, 3 to 4 minutes on the flip side. Remove steaks from the pan and let sit for 5 minutes before slicing into very thin serving pieces

This dish may be served on skewers as an appetizer. As an entrée, it is excellent with mashed new red potatoes or julienne fried potatoes.

Presentation: Place potatoes in center of plate. Arrange sliced meat over potatoes. Pour sauce over meat and around the plate. Sauce may also be served on the side.

LE RELAIS
Chef Daniel Stage

Calvados and Tarragon Pork Tenderloin Medallions with Calvados Veal Stock Reduction

Serves 4

2 -1/2 pounds pork (2-1/2 to 3 ounce medallions)
1 tablespoon shallots, finely diced
1/2 cup Dijon mustard
3 tablespoons walnut oil
1 tablespoon tarragon, chopped
1/2 cup Calvados
1/4 cup heavy cream
Salt and pepper to taste
1 cup fava beans, cleaned and blanched (see below)
1 cup reduced veal stock (see below)
(or veal stock purchased from a gourmet specialty store)

Fingerling Potato Salad
1-1/2 pounds fingerling potatoes, medium diced
1/4 cup shallots, finely diced
1/4 cup lard or olive oil
1/4 cup red wine vinegar
2 tablespoons sugar
1 tablespoon Dijon mustard
2 tablespoons red onions, finely chopped
2 tablespoons parsley, chopped
2 tablespoons chives, snipped
1/2 pound bacon, julienned
Salt and pepper to taste

Veal Stock
5 pounds veal bones
1 large onion, peeled and quartered
1 large carrot, peeled and large diced
3 stalks celery, large diced
1 gallon cold water
3 black peppercorns
1 small by leaf
4 cups red wine

Marinate pork medallions in mustard for 6 to 8 hours.

Shell fava beans and discard pods. Remove skins and blanch beans. Then, slit the skin around one end. Press opposite end between your fingers and squeeze bean out of casing.

Marinate pork medallions. Sear on both sides, approximately 3 minutes or until crust forms. Remove pork from pan. Place in a pre-heated 350 degree oven for 6 to 8 minutes to finish. Add shallots to pan and deglaze with Calvados. Reduce by three-fourths. Add veal stock. Reduce heat and whisk in butter and cream. Finish with tarragon, fava beans and salt and pepper.

Veal Stock
Roast bones in a 400 degree oven for 30 - 40 minutes on a sheet pan. Remove bones from pan and place in stock pot on stove at low heat. Add onions to roasting pan and brown slightly over medium heat. Add celery and carrots. Deglaze with red wine. Combine all ingredients in stock pot. Simmer for 8 - 10 hours. Skim fat off top, then strain through a fine sieve. Place liquid back on stove to reduce by three fourths, or until liquid coats the back of a spoon.

Fingerling Potato Salad
Cook bacon and remove from pan. Add shallots to hot pan. Deglaze with red wine vinegar. Add sugar and mustard Let cool. Whisk in lard or olive oil. Toss potatoes, red onion, parsley, chives and bacon with dressing. Season with salt and pepper.

Roasted Prawns in Lobster Broth Reduction

4 servings

2 pounds prawns,
cleaned and marinated for 4 to 6 hours
12 middleneck clams
12 spears asparagus, peeled and blanched
4 Yukon Gold potatoes - tourner
(peeled and evenly cut)
1 bulb roasted fennel, quartered
1 quart lobster broth

Prawns Marinade
1/4 cup tarragon
3 cloves shallots
5 cloves garlic
1-1/4 cup olive oil

Blend all until smooth.

Roasted Fennel
3 whole fennel
1/4 pound butter
1/2 cup chicken stock (see below)
or prepared chicken broth
3 sprigs thyme
Salt

Chicken Stock
1-1/2 pounds chicken wings
1 large onion, peeled and roughly chopped
2 large carrots, peeled and roughly chopped
2 stalks celery, peeled and roughly chopped
1 bouquet garni
5 black peppercorns
1/2 gallon water

Lobster Broth
2 1/2 pounds whole lobsters*
2 carrots, medium diced
1/2 bunch celery, medium diced
2 onions, medium diced
1 cup tomato paste
3 sprigs tarragon
1 bay leaf
1-1/2 gallons chicken stock
1 cup brandy
2 ounces canola oil

Heat a large sauté pan with 2 tablespoons of olive oil. Add clams, then prawns. Cook for about 2 - 3 minutes. Add fennel, asparagus, potatoes and lobster broth. Arrange in bowl. Strain sauce through a chinois (a fine mesh strainer) over top of prawns. Serve immediately.

Roasted Fennel
Heat butter in a saucepan. Add fennel. Rotate until brown. Add chicken stock and thyme. Cover with foil and bake at 350 degrees for 45 minutes or until tender.

Chicken Stock
Rinse chicken wings. Place in pan with remaining ingredients and bring to a boil. Simmer for 2 to 3 hours, skimming often. Strain stock. Then refrigerate for up to 3 days.

Lobster Broth
Caramelize carrots, onions and celery. In a separate pan, smoking hot, add canola oil. Cook lobsters for 5 to 10 minutes. Then add caramelized onions, mirepoix (carrots, celery and onions). Coat with tomato paste and mix together. Deglaze with brandy. Add chicken stock, tarragon and bay leaf. Simmer for 1 to 2 hours. Strain through a chinois.

*Some chefs recommend placing the live lobster in the freezer for an hour to desensitize it before killing. Or, ask your seafood supplier if they can provide ready lobsters.

Slow-Roasted Lamb Shanks with Mediterranean Sauce and Creamy Grits with Chevre

Serves 4

4 lamb shanks
3 tablespoons Dijon mustard
1 tablespoon fresh thyme, chopped
1/2 teaspoon cracked pepper
6 tablespoons olive oil
1-1/2 cups dry white wine
1 tablespoon garlic, finely chopped
1 cup shallots, thinly sliced
1 tablespoon anchovies, chopped
1 tablespoon capers
1/2 cup green cracked Spanish olives, pitted and sliced
1 tablespoon fresh parsley, chopped
2 cups fresh tomatoes, chopped
3 cups chicken stock

Preheat oven to 250 degrees.

Rub the shanks with the Dijon, thyme and cracked pepper. Marinate 24 to 48 hours.

Heat 3 tablespoons olive oil in a skillet. Braise the shanks on all sides. Remove from skillet and place in a roasting pan. Deglaze with 1/2 cup wine and pour over shanks.

Add remaining olive oil to skillet. Toss in garlic and shallots, and cook until golden. Deglaze with remaining wine and add anchovies, capers, olives, parsley, tomatoes and stock. Bring to a boil; pour over shanks. Cover and bake at 250 degrees for 3 hours.

Remove shanks and reduce sauce by half. Spoon sauce over shanks and serve with creamy grits.

Creamy Grits with Chevre
4 cups salted water
1-1/4 cup organic grits
3 tablespoons butter
4 ounces soft chevre
Cayenne pepper, to taste

Bring salted water to a boil. Reduce heat and slowly whisk in the grits. Cook for 8 minutes, then add butter, chevre and cayenne to taste. Serve immediately.

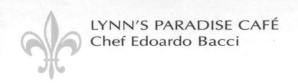
Chicken Kentuckian

Serves 4

Four 6-ounce boneless chicken breasts
1/4 cup flour
2 tablespoons olive oil
1 tablespoon butter
2 tablespoons shallots, minced
1 cup button mushrooms, sliced
1/4 cup bourbon
2 cups heavy cream
1 cup baby spinach
1 tablespoon thyme, minced
1/2 teaspoon freshly ground black pepper
Salt to taste

Dredge chicken breasts in flour and set aside.

Heat 2 tablespoons olive oil in a large sauté pan over medium high heat. Add floured chicken breasts and lightly season with salt and pepper. Sauté 3 to 4 minutes on each side or until golden brown. They should be about 3/4 done. Set aside and keep warm.

Heat 1 tablespoon of butter in the same pan. Add the shallots and sauté until translucent, about 1 minute. Add mushrooms and stir well. Sauté for another minute.

Off the heat, carefully add the bourbon. Return to the heat. Bourbon will flame briefly.

Add the cream, baby spinach, and thyme. Mix well and simmer for about 2 minutes, until slightly reduced. Add the browned chicken breasts back into the pan. Bring to a high simmer and cook for 5 minutes, until sauce has thickened and chicken has finished cooking.

Season with salt to taste.

Serve immediately over orzo pasta or basmati rice.

Osso Bucco

Serves 4

4 veal shanks, center cut about 12 ounces each
2 tablespoons olive oil
1 cup flour
Salt, pepper and paprika to taste
3/4 cup carrots, finely diced
3/4 cup yellow onion, finely diced
3/4 cup celery, finely diced
1/4 teaspoon garlic, minced
6 Roma tomatoes, peeled, deseeded and diced
1/2 cup dry red wine
1 cup Espagnole sauce or canned brown gravy
1 teaspoon thyme
1/4 teaspoon fennel
2 tablespoons fresh parsley, chopped
Salt and pepper to taste

Combine flour with salt, pepper and paprika. Mix.

Heat olive oil in a sauté pan. Dredge veal shanks in seasoned flour and place in hot olive oil. Lightly sear all sides of veal until golden brown. Add vegetables and garlic and cook for 3 to 5 minutes longer. Then add tomatoes and deglaze with wine. Add Espagnole sauce or brown gravy, thyme, fennel, parsley, salt and pepper.

Place browned veal into a large, ovenproof baking dish and pour sauce/vegetable mixture over the top of the veal.

Preheat oven to 325 degrees and cover the veal dish. Bake for 4-1/2 to 5 hours, or until the veal is "fork tender" and starting to fall off the bone.

Gently remove the shanks from the pan with a slotted spoon and reserve.

Scrape the sauce out of the baking dish and place into the bowl of a food processor. Quickly pulse a few times. Pour the sauce over the veal and serve.

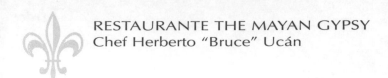
Salmon Tikin Xik

Serves 4

Four 7 ounce salmon fillets
2 ounces achiote paste mix
(available in specialty markets)
1/2 cup olive oil
1 tablespoon garlic, chopped
Salt to taste
1/2 cup dry white cooking wine or other wine
1 green bell pepper, julienned
1 medium purple onion, chopped
Juice of one orange
1 cup water
2 ounces butter
Juice of 1 lime
1 tablespoon vinegar
4 servings rice, prepared according to package directions

Achiote (Annatto) Sauce for Salmon: Dissolve achiote with water, orange juice, lime juice, vinegar and salt. Put this mixture in a sauce pan and heat to reduce to a sauce consistency. Add butter and wine. Set aside.

In another pan, sauté green pepper and onion in oil for 3 minutes. (Or, the onion and green pepper may be grilled, giving them a slightly charred appearance). Set aside.

Rub the salmon with the olive oil and chopped garlic, then sauté in a hot fry pan, or place under the broiler or on a grill for 5 minutes for medium.

For each serving, place rice on a plate. Top rice with salmon, any vegetables of your choice and Anchiote sauce.

SALSA SOUTH BEACH
Chef Marshall Jewell

Rum Marinated Pork Chop with Banana Chutney

I like to serve this dish with spicy rice and beans and my favorite vegetable, sugar snaps.

Serves 6

Six 12 ounce pork chops

Marinade
1/2 cup soy sauce
1/3 cup dark rum
1/3 cup onion, chopped
1 tablespoon fresh ginger, grated
1 clove garlic, minced

Banana Chutney
1/2 red pepper
1/2 yellow pepper
1 medium yellow onion
1 Fuji apple

2 ripe bananas
1 tablespoon lemon
1/2 teaspoon garlic, minced
1/3 cup apple cider vinegar
1/3 teaspoon salt
3/4 cup brown sugar
Pinch each of cloves, ginger, cinnamon
1 tablespoon each of chopped basil,
cilantro and parsley
Dash each of lemon juice and olive oil
Lime and cilantro to garnish

Before you marinate, reserve a small amount of the marinade to brush the chops during grilling.

To prepare the marinade: Mix ingredients and add pork chops. Marinate for about an hour in the refrigerator. Remove. Preheat grill or broiler and cook chops until done, about 15 minutes. Brush chops with marinade during grilling.

Place cooked chop on a plate and top with a generous amount of chutney. Garnish with lime and cilantro.

Banana Chutney
Dice in small pieces the peppers, onion, apple and bananas. Add the lemon juice. Mix well. Add the remaining ingredients. Mix well, cover and chill for one hour.

Duck Breast with Pomegranate Walnut Sauce

6 servings

6 duck breasts (or other fowl), skin removed
1/4 cup olive oil
1 tablespoon green peppercorns
1 cup onion, medium dice
1/2 cup walnuts, chopped fine
1 tablespoon tomato paste
1 tablespoon angelica, dried (optional)
1 teaspoon turmeric
1 teaspoon salt
1 teaspoon oregano
1 teaspoon thyme

1 teaspoon pepper
1 pinch cardamom
1 cup pomegranate juice
*(If pomegranate juice is not available, substitute
1/2 cup of balsamic vinegar. One tablespoon sugar
can be added to cut the sourness of the sauce)*
1-1/2 cups duck stock
(or homemade chicken stock or canned unsalted chicken broth)
3 tablespoons oil

In a bowl, place olive oil, peppercorns and duck breasts. Marinate in the refrigerator for 2 hours.

In a heavy sauce pan over medium heat, sauté onions until golden brown, about 5 minutes. Add walnuts, stirring constantly for 10 minutes. Add tomato paste and dried ingredients. Cook 10 minutes longer. Stir occasionally so mixture does not stick.

Add pomegranate juice. Cook until liquid has reduced by half. Add stock, reduce heat, and simmer for 45 minutes. Remove from heat and allow to cool. Purée mixture in a blender.

Heat a large sauté pan. Add oil and sear duck until light brown on all sides. Add sauce and simmer 10 minutes, or until duck reaches desired doneness.

Pork Chops and Apple Sauce

Serves 6

6 pork chops, any cut, at least 1" thick
2 quarts water
2 cups brown sugar
1 cup salt
3 bay leaves
2 tablespoons peppercorns

Combine all ingredients, except pork, in a pot. Bring to a boil. Remove from heat. Let cool. When cool, add pork and refrigerate for 2 hours. Remove pork from brine and drain. Cook on the grill or under the broiler to desired doneness.

Applesauce
4 Granny Smith apples,
peeled, seeded and roughly chopped
2 tablespoons onion, minced
1 tablespoon cider vinegar
1 tablespoon brown sugar
1 teaspoon ginger, chopped
Pinch cinnamon
1 teaspoon Dijon mustard
1 teaspoon lime juice
Pinch dried sage

Combine all ingredients and simmer on low heat until light brown and thick, about 2 hours. Serve with mashed potatoes and fresh seasonal vegetables.

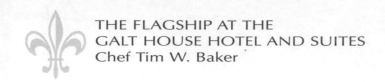

Sautéed Grouper with Braised Napa Cabbage and Shitake Soy Glaze

Serves 4

Grouper
1/4 cup olive oil
2 pounds grouper, cut into four 8 ounce portions
Salt and pepper
All purpose flour to dredge

Braised Napa Cabbage
3 tablespoons butter
2 cloves garlic, chopped
2 tablespoons fresh ginger, finely chopped
1 head Napa cabbage, cut into 1" slices
1 red pepper, julienned
1 yellow pepper, julienned
1 large carrot, julienned
1 bunch cilantro, chopped (reserve stems for sauce)
1 cup chicken stock
Salt and pepper

Shitake Soy Glaze
2 tablespoons butter
2 cups shitake mushrooms, sliced
1/2 cup shallots, roughly chopped
1/4 cup ginger, roughly chopped
2 cloves garlic, roughly chopped
1/2 cup sherry
Cilantro stems
2 cups water
1/2 cup soy sauce
1 tablespoon Chinese chile sauce
1/4 cup honey
Salt and pepper

Heat olive oil in a heavy bottom 10" skillet over medium high heat. Season grouper with salt and pepper. Dredge in flour and shake off excess. Place 2 fillets in skillet and sauté 3 minutes on each side, or until they have a nice golden crust. Repeat with remaining fillets. Place grouper in a 350 degree oven for 3 minutes until cooked through.

Braised Napa Cabbage
Melt butter in a large pot over medium heat. Add ginger and garlic and cook for 1 minute. Add the vegetables and cook for 4 minutes. Add chicken stock. Cover and simmer for 10 minutes until cabbage is just tender. Season with salt and pepper to taste.

Shitake Soy Glaze
Melt 1 tablespoon butter in another medium saucepan over medium heat. Add shallots, ginger and garlic. Sauté for 2 minutes until soft. Deglaze pan with sherry. Add remaining ingredients and simmer for 15 minutes until sauce starts to thicken. Strain sauce and add to shiitakes. May need to be thickened with a small amount of cornstarch and water.

Assembly
Divide cabbage onto four plates. Place grouper on top of cabbage. Top with glaze and mushrooms.

Roasted Rack of Lamb

Serves 6

3 racks of lamb, frenched
Salt and black pepper, as needed
2 tablespoons olive oil
2 tablespoons unsalted butter
Pinch cayenne pepper

Season the lamb with the salt, black pepper and cayenne pepper. Place an oven-proof sauté pan on high heat. Once the pan reaches a high temperature, add the oil. Sear the lamb on both sides until well browned. Add the butter and place in a 400 degree oven, meat side down. Roast for 10 to 12 minutes. Allow the lamb to rest for another 4 to 5 minutes before slicing.

Maple and Walnut Risotto

Serves 8

4 tablespoons unsalted butter
2 tablespoons olive oil
1 medium onion, finely diced
2 cups arborio rice
3 cups chicken stock or warmed broth
1/4 cup dry roasted walnuts
1/4 cup pure maple syrup
1/4 cup Parmesan cheese, grated
Salt and pepper to taste

Heat 2 tablespoons of the butter and the oil in a heavy sauce pan over low heat. Add the onions and cook them, stirring occasionally, until they are tender and golden in color. Stir the rice into the pan and turn the heat up to medium, stirring continuously for 3 to 5 minutes.

Pour one quarter of the hot chicken broth into the pan and allow it to come to a simmer, stirring continuously until all of the liquid is absorbed. Repeat this process two times. Add the walnuts and maple syrup. Stir and add the last quarter of the broth while stirring continuously. Remove the sauce pan from the heat and finish the risotto by adding in the rest of the butter along with the Parmesan cheese. Season with salt and pepper.

Remember: The rice will continue to absorb liquid as it stands, so be generous with the final addition of broth.

Fresh Mozzarella and Prosciutto Stuffed French Veal Chop with Morel Marsala Sauce

Serves 1

1/2 cup olive oil
1/4 cup Parmesan cheese, grated
One 10 ounce fresh veal chop
1 slice fresh mozzarella
1 cup panko (Japanese bread crumbs)
seasoned with salt and pepper
1 egg, beaten
1 cup flour
1 slice prosciutto

Mix flour with salt and pepper to taste.

Cut a small slit in the chop by the upper part of the bone and work down about one inch. Stuff chop with mozzarella and prosciutto.

Dredge chop through seasoned flour, then coat with egg. Crust with a mixture of Parmesan cheese and panko. Press firmly so crumbs stick well to chop. Heat skillet, add oil, and brown chops on both sides. Finish chop in oven at 350 degrees until it reaches an internal temperature of 165 degrees. Remove from oven. Serve.

Morel Marsala Sauce
2 ounces dried morel mushrooms (reconstituted)
1 ounce Marsala
1 tablespoon olive oil
1 small shallot, minced
Salt and pepper
1 cup heavy whipping cream
1 teaspoon fresh chives, chopped fine

Morel Marsala Sauce
In a sauce pan, heat oil and shallots. Cook until transparent, then add mushrooms and Marsala. Add salt and pepper to taste. Let alcohol cook out of Marsala. Add whipping cream and reduce by half. Add chives. Pour sauce over chop.

Braised Chicken with Local Organic Mushrooms

Serves 7

4 tablespoons canola oil
7 pieces organic chicken
1-1/2 pounds wild mushrooms
(a mix of oyster and shitake)
4 tablespoons garlic, chopped
1 bunch leeks, chopped
1/2 cup barley
1/2 cup Arborio rice
4 cups chicken stock
3-1/2 cups Cabernet Sauvignon or Syrah
2 tablespoons fresh thyme, chopped
1 tablespoon fresh rosemary, chopped
1 bay leaf
Sea salt to taste
Cracked black pepper to taste

Heat oil in a sauté pan and add chicken. Sear until brown on each side.

Remove chicken onto a plate. Wipe pan clean and add 3 tablespoons of canola oil and leeks. Cook until caramelized. Add mushrooms. After mushrooms have wilted, stir in the barley and risotto and begin to toast the grains. When you have achieved a nutty smell, add the red wine and reduce by half. Then add 1/2 of the chicken stock. Cook on low heat and stir continuously with a wooden spoon. Once it has absorbed almost all of the stock, add the remaining liquid, herbs and salt and pepper. Stir until a bit of the stock has absorbed, then place chicken on top. Cover and simmer on stovetop or place in a 350 degree oven. Just add more liquid if anything begins to stick to the pan. Cooking time may vary upon the size of the chicken and if you choose to use boneless chicken. But, chicken should be very tender. Cool and reheat if needed.

Cioppino 211

Serves 4

3/4 cup unsalted butter
Splash of olive oil
1 small onion, julienned
4 cloves garlic minced
1 bulb fennel, sliced
Pinch saffron
1 cup canned Italian tomatoes,
preferably San Marzano
1/2 pound orzo pasta
12 littleneck clams
12 fresh 16-20 count shrimp,
Royal Red if available

4 softshell crabs, if available
3/4 pound striped bass or black sea bass filet
3/4 pound monkfish filet
1 tablespoon parsley, chopped
1 tablespoon chives, chopped
1 tablespoon chervil, chopped
1 teaspoon grated orange zest
1 lemon
Salt and pepper to taste
1/8 cup grapeseed oil
Eight u-10 dayboat or diver scallops

1 quart fish stock
(you may substitute clam juice)

5 pounds of fish bones and trimmings of white fish
(snapper, sole, turbot etc.)
(ask your fish monger for bones and trimmings)
1 onion, sliced
2 shallots, sliced
2 stalks celery, sliced

Fennel tops from one bulb, sliced
2 bay leaves
1 sprig thyme
1/2 lemon
10 cups cold water
2 cups white wine

When preparing this dish it is very important to find the freshest seafood available.

To prepare the fish stock: Peel and slice the onions, shallots, celery, and fennel top. Put in a stock pot along with the fish bones and trimmings, bay leaves, thyme, lemon, water and wine. Slowly bring the liquid to a boil, skim the top and boil gently for 30 minutes. Strain through a fine mesh strainer and set aside.

Put a saucepan on medium heat and add 1/4 cup of butter then add the onions, garlic, and fennel. When the vegetables start to sweat add a good pinch of saffron. Keep cooking for a couple more minutes, then crush the tomatoes into the pot and add 4 cups of fish stock. Let simmer uncovered until it is reduced by a third. Set aside

While the sauce is simmering, boil water and cook the orzo pasta. Remove and drain. Season, toss in

oil and put aside. Put a large sauté pan on medium high heat and add 1/4 cup of butter with a splash of olive oil so the butter doesn't burn. Add the clams, then the shrimp, soft shell crabs, if they are available, the bass, and monkfish. Pour sauce in and cover until the clams and mussels open. Then, uncover and add chopped herbs, orange zest, splash of lemon juice, and salt and pepper to taste.

In a separate, smoking hot pan, add the grapeseed oil, then the scallops. Leave on one side until they turn a nice color, then turn and brown the other side, keeping them medium rare. Set on platters.

Presentation: Evenly divide the fish and sauce between four large deep oval platters or large bowls. Put a small spoonful of orzo pasta in the center of the dish and garnish with a fresh sprig of chervil.

UPTOWN CAFÉ
Chef Matt Weber

Spicy Grilled Quail Wrapped with Zucchini with Marinated Grilled Asparagus and Smoked Gouda Corncakes

Serves 6

12 semi boned quail
Bean paste marinade (see below)
4 to 5 zucchini, sliced into 1/8" strips lengthwise
Kosher salt and freshly ground black pepper, to taste

Korean Bean Paste Marinade

6 tablespoons Korean bean paste
3 cloves garlic, minced
4 tablespoons ginger, minced
1 bunch green onions, chopped
1/2 cup soy sauce
1/2 cup corn oil
2 tablespoons sesame oil

Raspberry Ketchup

2 tablespoons corn oil
One 12 ounce package frozen raspberries
4 teaspoons yellow onions, diced
1 clove garlic, minced
1 tablespoon ginger root, minced
4 tablespoons light brown sugar
1/4 teaspoon ground cloves
1/4 teaspoon cinnamon
Cayenne pepper to taste
2 teaspoons dried mint
Salt to taste
4 tablespoons raspberry red wine vinegar
2/3 cup chicken stock or broth
1 tablespoon cornstarch
2 tablespoons water

To prepare marinade for quail: Mix first 5 ingredients together in a large bowl. Whisk oils in last. Place quail in bowl and gently toss to coat quail evenly with marinade. Set aside. Hint: Finish this step at least 1/2 hour before grilling or broiling quail.

To prepare zucchini: Drop zucchini slices into boiling water and cook until barely tender. Remove immediately and drop zucchini into ice water. Drain and sprinkle with salt and pepper. Set aside.

Preheat grill or broiler. Remove quail from marinade. Grill or broil the quail 5 to 6 minutes on one side. Turn and broil about the same time on the other side. Check to be sure they're done before you remove them from the grill or broiler. Set aside to cool.

Gently wrap zucchini slices around quail and very gently knot the zucchini. Place the quail back on the grill or under broiler until zucchini is slightly charred.

On each serving plate, fan out the grilled asparagus and place two corncakes on each side of the plate. Set one quail on each cake. Drizzle entire plate with raspberry ketchup. Garnish with a sprig of fresh mint.

Raspberry Ketchup

In a medium to heavy weight sauce pan, sauté onion, garlic and ginger. Add all other ingredients except cornstarch and water. Simmer approximately 5 to 10 minutes. Strain. Press raspberries through, trying to remove seeds. Put strained mixture back on the heat.

Mix cornstarch and water to make a slurry. Stir. Add to hot raspberry sauce. Check to be sure that the consistency is correct. It should coat the back of a spoon. Check for taste and add more salt, if needed.

See next page for accompanying dishes.

Marinated Grilled Asparagus

2 bunches asparagus, bottoms trimmed
2 teaspoons freshly ground black pepper
1 tablespoon dried or 2 tablespoons fresh thyme
1 tablespoon garlic chile sauce
2 cloves garlic, minced
Juice of 2 lemons
2 teaspoons kosher salt
1/2 cup raspberry red wine vinegar
2/3 cup extra virgin olive oil

Preheat grill. Set aside asparagus in a wide, shallow dish. Combine garlic, chile sauce, salt, pepper, thyme, lemon juice and vinegar. Whisk in olive oil and pour over asparagus. Grill asparagus until slightly charred and tender.

Hint: Grill asparagus just before finishing quail. Set asparagus aside.

Smoked Gouda Corncakes

Makes about 15 one ounce corncakes

3/4 cup all purpose flour, sifted
2-1/2 teaspoons double acting baking powder
3/4 teaspoon salt
3/4 teaspoon cayenne pepper
1-1/4 cup yellow or white stone ground cornmeal
1 egg, slightly beaten

1 cup buttermilk
2 tablespoons butter, melted
1 cup smoked Gouda, grated
2 green onions, diced
2 ears fresh corn, kernels only
6 tablespoons red bell pepper, diced

Sift all dry ingredients together into a large bowl. Beat in egg, buttermilk and butter. Stir in remaining ingredients. Fry as you would pancakes in a medium skillet or on a griddle. Remove and keep warm in a 200 degree oven until ready to serve.

Hint: Test one cake for batter consistency and temperature of cooking surface. Adjust accordingly.

Bocconcini Di Vitello
(Roulade of Veal)

Serves 2

4 slices of veal scaloppine (2 ounces each slice)
8 pieces of prosciutto, thinly sliced
8 slices fontina cheese (approximately 6 ounces total)
16 leaves fresh sage
1/2 cup dry white wine
1/2 cup veal stock or chicken broth
1/4 cup all purpose flour
3 tablespoons butter
Salt and pepper
Fresh parsley
Carrots, julienned (optional for garnish)

Pound veal to 1/8" thick and cut each piece in half (or have butcher do this for you). Lay veal flat. Layer the prosciutto on top of veal, then add fontina on top of prosciutto. Neither prosciutto nor fontina should extend the entire length of the veal. Top the fontina with a leaf of sage and roll the veal lengthwise. Dust the finished roulades with the flour.

If using carrots as a garnish, lightly sauté them in about 1 tablespoon of butter. Set aside.

Melt 1 tablespoon butter in a skillet. Place the veal in the skillet over low heat. Roll the veal around in the skillet to cook evenly. Remove veal from the skillet. Pour the wine into the skillet along with 8 leaves of sage and veal stock. Add 1 tablespoon of butter and cook over l low heat for 2 to 3 minutes.

Arrange veal on each plate. Strain sauce and pour over veal. Sprinkle with fresh parsley or finely julienned carrots. Serve.

Stir Fry of Veal with Enoki Mushrooms, Peapods and Torn Pasta Finished with Oyster Sauce and Pistachio Oil

Serves 1

1 tablespoon butter
1/2 package of Enoki mushrooms
3 to 4 ounces of veal, julienned
1 tablespoon Marsala
5 wonton sheets, cut on the diagonal
8 to 10 pieces red pepper, julienned
10 to 12 sugar snap peas, cut on bias
1 teaspoon soy sauce
1 teaspoon oyster sauce
2 drops sesame oil
2 tablespoons heavy cream
2 teaspoons pistachio nuts, chopped
1/2 teaspoon pistachio oil

Place a saucepan on high heat and add butter. Allow butter to brown and add the mushrooms and the veal. Allow to caramelize slightly. Deglaze the pan with the Marsala. Add the torn pasta, peppers and sugar snap peas. Add the remainder of the liquids and reduce slightly.

Serve mounded in a bowl. Finish with pistachios and pistachio oil.

Desserts

Dessert can be a light and refreshing end to a meal. Or, it can be a decadently rich surprise. And, of course, for special occasions, dessert can be the grand finale! Louisville's celebrated chefs share their repertoire of sweet concoctions for you and your guests to enjoy.

ASIATIQUE
Chef Peng S. Looi

Malaysian Style Tapioca Pearls with Honeydew

Serves 4

3/4 cup tapioca pearls
6 cups water
1 slice ginger
1 cup coconut milk (evaporated milk can be substituted)
1/2 cup sugar
1/2 honeydew (fruit salad can be substituted)

Soak tapioca pearls in 2 cups of water for 30 minutes. Drain. Bring the remaining 4 cups of water to a boil and add the drained tapioca. Cook until transparent. Drain in a sieve and wash under cold running water. Set aside until cool.

Boil sugar, 1/2 cup water and ginger for 20 minutes until it reaches a syrupy consistency. Remove from heat and cool.

Peel and seed honeydew. Cut into small cubes or make small balls with a melon baller. Mix the tapioca, coconut milk, honeydew cubes and syrup. Chill. Serve.

Individual Fried Apple Cheesecakes

When I moved to Kentucky, I had my first Fried Apple Pie in Casey County. I thought it was one of the best things I had ever tasted. This dessert is a Kentucky country tradition that I played with and turned into our most popular dessert at Avalon. I use shortbread rather than pie dough, fill it with cream cheese and apple butter, and fry it. I serve it with vanilla ice cream and load it up with apple caramel. It is so good with that "State Fair" kind of feel.

Serves 6

Dough*
2 cups all purpose flour
6-1/2 tablespoons sugar
1 tablespoon baking powder
1 teaspoon baking soda
1/4 teaspoon salt
1/2 cup butter, partially softened
1 egg
1/2 cup buttermilk
Vanilla ice cream

Cream Cheese Filling
4 ounces cream cheese, softened
2 tablespoons sugar
1 tablespoon apple butter

Caramel Apple Sauce
1 cup sugar
1 tablespoon water
1 cup heavy cream
1 tablespoon vanilla
1 Granny Smith apple, peeled and diced

Dough
Stir the dry ingredients together in a large mixing bowl until well blended. Add the butter by pressing it into the flour with your fingers and palms until it is grainy and crumbly. This is a 10 to 15 minute process.

Lightly whisk the egg and milk, then gradually add to the flour mixture, stirring with a rubber spatula until a sticky, well blended dough forms. Chill completely for 3 to 4 hours.

Remove from refrigerator and form into 3-ounce balls and roll out into 4" rounds on a floured surface. Drop 2 tablespoons of the cream cheese filling into the center of each round. Brush with egg wash and fold into an empanada shape. Seal with a fork. Cover and freeze.

Remove cheesecakes from freezer and fry at 400 degrees until they start to brown and the juices start to release. Top with one scoop of vanilla ice cream and 2 to 3 ounces of caramel applesauce.

Cream Cheese Filling
Mix all ingredients in a food processor until smooth. Set aside.

Caramel Apple Sauce
Cook the sugar and water over medium high heat, stirring frequently until it dissolves and starts developing an amber color. This takes around 10 minutes.

Reduce heat to medium and slowly add the cream while stirring constantly. Be very careful when you add the cream because it will start to boil and bubble rapidly. It may even turn hard for a few seconds. Just remember to go slowly and be careful.

After the cream has been incorporated, allow the caramel to reduce slightly at a slow boil over medium heat for 8 to 10 minutes.

Add the vanilla and the diced apple. Serve warm.

Placed a cheesecake on a plate. Top with a generous scoop of vanilla ice cream and ladle apple caramel over the ice cream. Garnish with whipped cream and mint, if desired. Repeat with remaining servings.

*This dough freezes really well. You may want to portion and freeze the remaining dough according to your needs. You could even make a few extra apple cheesecakes and freeze them for later use.

BAXTER STATION BAR AND GRILL
Chef Tom Jackson

Peaches and Cream

My favorite desserts are the most simple and light. This is one of my favorites. It's simple but very, very good.

Serves 4

3 ripe peaches, peeled, pitted and medium diced, refrigerated
1/2 quart heavy cream
2 tablespoons powdered sugar
1 tablespoon Triple Sec liqueur

In a stainless steel bowl, using a thin whisk, whip cream by hand until it sets up. (This should only take five mintues, tops). Be careful not to overwhip the cream until it becomes buttery. Add the powdered sugar and the Triple Sec. Place in another bowl and refrigerate.

When ready to serve, fold the peaches into the cream. Divide into four martini glasses and serve.

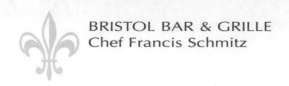

French Bread Pudding with Bourbon Sauce

Serves 4 to 6

French Bread Pudding
2 cups warm water
1-1/2 cups sugar
1 can evaporated milk
One 12 ounce loaf of French bread, torn into bite size pieces
1/2 teaspoon vanilla extract
1/2 cup raisins
Pinch of nutmeg
5 eggs, lightly beaten
6 tablespoons unsalted butter, melted

French Bread Pudding

In a bowl, dissolve sugar in warm water. Stir in milk, melted butter, raisins, nutmeg and eggs. Stir bread into liquid mixture. Let mixture sit for about 45 minutes, stirring occasionally. Pour into a greased 9" x 13" pan and bake in a 375 degree pre-heated oven until golden brown, about 35 minutes. Serve with Bourbon Sauce.

Bourbon Sauce
1 cup light Karo Syrup
1/4 stick unsalted butter, melted
1/4 cup bourbon
1/2 teaspoon vanilla extract

Mix all ingredients together in a small saucepan and heat until warmed.

BUCK'S
Chef Gerard Hampton

Key Lime Pie

6 to 8 servings

One 9" prepared graham cracker shell
One 14 ounce can condensed milk
3 egg yolks
1/2 cup key lime juice

Whipped cream for garnish

Place the milk, egg yolks and lime juice in a mixing bowl and whip for 5 minutes.

Pour the mixture into the pie shell and bake for 15 minutes at 350 degrees. Remove from oven and let cool for 10 minutes. Place the pie in the refrigerator for 1 to 2 hours.

Before serving, top with whipped cream.

Banana Poppyseed Guggelhopf

Serves 8

1 stick of butter, left at room temperature for 15 minutes
2 cups cake flour
2 teaspoons baking powder
1 cup powdered sugar
4 eggs, at room temperature
1 cup ripe bananas, mashed
3 tablespoons Frangelica liqueur
1/3 cup heavy cream
1/4 cup poppyseeds
1 teaspoon vanilla
3/4 cup brown sugar

Preheat oven to 350 degrees. Butter or spray the inside of a 9" to 9-1/2" Guggelhopf mold or Bundt pan. Dust with flour.

In a medium bowl, beat the butter until you have a smooth cream texture. Gradually add powdered sugar in three parts. Beat until pale and smooth. Then, beat in eggs one at a time until thoroughly mixed.

In another bowl, sift together cake flour, baking powder and salt. In another bowl, mix brown sugar, bananas, heavy cream, Frangelica and vanilla until all ingredients are fully incorporated into mixture. Add flour mixture to banana mixture in three separate steps, mixing well each time.

Pour into pan and bake 45 to 55 minutes or until a cake tester or toothpick pulls out clean. Let sit 10 minutes. Invert pan and remove cake.

EL MUNDO
Chef Bea Chamberlain

El Mundo's Flan

Serves 4

Caramel
3/4 cup sugar
1/2 cup water

2 quarts milk
1 cup sugar
1 tablespoon vanilla
2 eggs
2 egg yolks

Preheat oven to 325 degrees.

In a clean, dry sauté pan, stir together 3/4 cup of the sugar and the water. Bring to a boil, then turn the heat down to medium. Do not stir anymore. Do not let it burn. When it starts to turn amber in color, you may swirl the pan to make it uniform. Divide this caramel into four 8 ounce ramekins, about 1/4 inch caramel in each ramekin.

While the sugar and water are cooking, combine in a heavy bottom pot the milk, sugar and vanilla. Cook and reduce by half.

While the milk mixture is cooking, mix together in a stainless steel bowl, the eggs and egg yolks. Set aside.

When the milk is reduced, whisk, little by little, the hot milk into the eggs. Always whisk hot into cold, and whisk like crazy. If you don't, the eggs will be like scrambled eggs. Strain this mixture through a fine mesh sieve and pour into the sugared ramekins. Bake at 325 degrees in a water bath (place ramekins in a square Pyrex dish and fill with about 1" of water) for 1-1/2 hours, checking each half hour to make sure they are not browning on top. If they are, turn the oven down by 25 degrees.

Note: The low heat is the key to a custardy, rather than a scrambled, bubbly end product.

Bourbon Chocolate Pecan Tart

Serves 6

3 eggs
1 cup dark Karo syrup
1 cup sugar
1/3 cup semisweet chocolate, chopped
2 tablespoons unsalted butter, melted
2 teaspoons vanilla
1-1/2 cup pecan halves
1 pie crust (9"), unbaked
1 ounce bourbon

In a large bowl, mix the eggs, syrup, sugar, chocolate, melted butter and vanilla. Mix until well blended. Add the pecans.

Pour mixture into pie shell and bake at 350 degrees for 50 - 60 minutes until done. Cook on a sheet pan in case it boils over. As soon as you remove the pie from the oven, sprinkle the bourbon over the top of the pie. Allow to cool. Serve.

Serve with whipped cream seasoned with bourbon, powdered sugar and a sprig of mint.

**EQUUS RESTAURANT/
JACK'S LOUNGE**
Pastry Chef Rebecca Johnson

Chocolate Orbit

Serves 8

*8 ounces butter
12 ounces bittersweet chocolate, chopped
6 eggs
1 cup sugar*

Preheat oven to 350 degrees. Butter and flour a 9" x 2" baking pan.

Melt butter and chocolate in a double boiler, whisking occasionally. In a medium bowl, whisk together eggs and sugar. Thoroughly whisk in melted chocolate. Pour into pan and cover tightly with aluminum foil. Bake until cake appears to have set, about 1 hour.

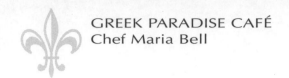
Baklava

Serves 10 – 14

1 pound walnuts, ground in a food processor
1/2 teaspoon cinnamon
1/2 teaspoon ground cloves
2 cups sugar
1 cup water
2 cups honey
2 sticks unsalted butter
1 package of Krinos or Athens phyllo dough

Melt butter. Carefully open the package of the phyllo dough. Working with two sheets at a time, place phyllo dough in a baking pan so that the dough lies flat. After you have placed two sheets in the pan, use a pastry brush to brush butter onto the top of the sheet. Repeat this procedure until you have used half a box of phyllo dough. Spread walnuts over last sheet in the pan. Sprinkle cinnamon and cloves over the top.

Continue layering the phyllo dough in the pan, again working with two sheets at a time, until you have used the entire box. Using a bread knife or other serrated knife, cut the baklava diagonally. Place pan in the oven and bake at 350 degrees until golden brown. Remove from oven and set aside.

Mix honey, water and sugar in a small saucepan. Slowly bring to a boil, stirring constantly until thick. Remove and set aside.

After pan and syrup both cool to room temperature, pour the syrup over the baked phyllo. Serve.

JACK FRY'S RESTAURANT
Pastry Chef Robyn Ferguson

Desserts

Key Lime White Chocolate Mousse Torte with Blackberry Sauce

Serves 12 – 16

Lime Shortbread Cookie Crust
4 tablespoons cold unsalted sweet butter
1/4 cup sugar
1/2 cup flour
Pinch of salt
Zest of 1 lime

Key Lime White Chocolate Mousse
16 ounces white chocolate
(Lindt or Callebaut)
3/4 cup key lime juice,
(preferably Aunt Nellie and Uncle Joe's)
Zest of 1 lime
3 cups heavy whipping cream

2 tablespoons unflavored gelatin
1/3 cup water
Pinch of cinnamon
Pinch of nutmeg
2 teaspoons vanilla

Blackberry Sauce
4 cups blackberries
(frozen berries may be used if fresh ones are not available)
Pinch salt
1 tablespoon fresh lemon juice
8 tablespoon granulated sugar
1/2 tablespoon blackberry liqueur

Lime Shortbread Cookie Crust
Preheat oven to 325 degrees. Cream the butter, sugar and lime zest in the bowl of an electric mixer using the paddle attachment. Mix on low for 15 seconds. Add the flour and salt and mix until the dough comes together.

Pat dough into the bottom of a 10" springform pan. Bake at 325 degrees until lightly browned. Cool to room temperature.

Key Lime White Chocolate Mousse
Combine white chocolate and key lime juice in the top of a double boiler until melted and smooth. Remove from heat and cool to room temperature.

Sprinkle gelatin over 1/3 cup of water. Let stand for 10 minutes until softened. Microwave gelatin 5 to 10 seconds until melted. Pour gelatin into electric mixing bowl. Add heavy whipping cream and vanilla. Using whisk attachment, beat cream to soft peaks. Fold whipped cream mixture into white chocolate mixture. Add cinnamon and nutmeg. Pour filling into crust and refrigerate overnight or until filling is set.

Blackberry Sauce
In a food processor, puree berries and granulated sugar. Strain puree through a strainer to eliminate seeds. To the mixture, stir in salt, lemon juice and liqueur. Refrigerate until ready to serve.

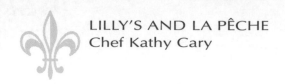

Pumpkin Cheesecake

Serves 12

Crust
2 cups graham cracker crumbs
1/4 cup sugar
1 tablespoon cinnamon
4 ounces butter, melted

Mix ingredients well in a 10" springform pan. Press to pan. Bake for 15-20 minutes at 350 degrees.

Filling
1-1/2 pounds cream cheese, softened
1 cup sugar
2 cups canned pumpkin
3 eggs
1 tablespoon cinnamon
1 teaspoon allspice
1 teaspoon nutmeg
1 teaspoon ginger

Put cream cheese and sugar in a food processor and process until smooth. Add pumpkin and pulse. Add eggs. Mix but do not overmix or cheesecake will soufflé. Add spices and pulse. Pour into the pre-baked crust. Cook for 30 minutes at 350 degrees or until sides crack. Cool.

Topping
3 cups sour cream
1 tablespoon cinnamon
3 ounces sugar
4 teaspoons vanilla

Mix ingredients and pour onto cooled cheesecake. Bake for 5 minutes in a 350 degree oven. Chill for 5 hours or overnight.

LYNN'S PARADISE CAFÉ
Chef Edoardo Bacci

Bourbon Ball French Toast

Serves 6

Batter
6 eggs
1-1/4 cups milk
1/2 teaspoon nutmeg
1/4 teaspoon cinnamon
1/8 teaspoon salt
1 teaspoon vanilla

One 1 pound loaf firm textured bread,
preferably a bâtarde or baguette
Butter or oil for frying

Bourbon Vanilla Custard
Yield: 1-3/4 cups

1 cup half and half
1/2 cup whipping cream
2 large egg yolks
1/4 cup sugar
2 teaspoons cornstarch
1 teaspoon vanilla extract
3 tablespoons Kentucky bourbon

Kentucky Bourbon Whipped Cream
2 cups heavy whipping cream
3 tablespoons powdered sugar
3 tablespoons Kentucky bourbon

Beat all batter ingredients together in a medium-sized bowl. Set aside.

Slice bâtarde into 1-inch thick slices. Soak the slices in the batter for about 3 minutes. Melt butter or oil in a sauté pan over medium heat. Lift the bread from the batter and place in a hot pan. Add only enough bread to fit easily in the pan. Sauté on both sides until golden brown. Keep warm until all slices have been cooked.

Place 2 or 3 slices on each plate. Drizzle with warm Bourbon Vanilla Custard.

Garnish with Hershey's or other Chocolate syrup and Kentucky Bourbon Whipped Cream. Sprinkle with toasted pecans. Serve immediately.

Bourbon Vanilla Custard
In a small saucepan, heat the half and half and whipping cream and bring to a boil. Meanwhile, whisk egg yolks, sugar and cornstarch in a stainless steel bowl for about 2 minutes or until mixture thickens and lightens in color. Slowly pour hot cream into the egg mixture, whisking constantly. Return the custard to the saucepan and place over medium heat. Stir constantly until the mixture reaches 180 degrees F. Remove from heat. Serve immediately or hold over a hot water bath.

Kentucky Bourbon Whipped Cream
Whip cream in well-chilled mixing bowl just until stiff peaks form. Add powdered sugar and bourbon and whip just long enough to incorporate. Taste and adjust flavors.

Italian Cream Cake

Serves 12

1/2 cup butter
1/2 cup shortening
1 pound sugar
5 egg yolks
1 pound flour, sifted
1 teaspoon baking soda
1 cup buttermilk
1 teaspoon vanilla
1/2 cup coconut
1 cup pecans, chopped
5 egg whites

Frosting
1 pound cream cheese, softened
3/4 cup butter, softened
4 cups powdered sugar
2 teaspoons vanilla

Grease and flour two 9" round cake pans or a 9" x 13" cake pan.

Cream butter and shortening in the bowl of a mixer. Add sugar, then egg yolks.

Beat egg whites until they form stiff peaks.

In a medium mixing bowl, stir baking soda into buttermilk. Add alternately with the flour to the creamed butter mixture. Add vanilla, coconut and pecans. Fold in egg whites.

Bake at 350 degrees for 35 minutes, or until a toothpick inserted in the middle of the cake comes out clean. Remove from oven and cool for 10 minutes. Run a knife around the edge of the pan. Invert cake onto a plate. Frost when completely cool.

Frosting
Whip cream cheese and butter in the bowl of a mixer. Add powdered sugar and vanilla. Spread onto cake.

SHARIAT'S
Chef Anoosh Shariat

White Chocolate Pumpkin Cheesecake

Serves 12

For the crust
Twelve 6" round corn tortillas (packaged)
1-1/2 cups sugar
2 tablespoons cinnamon
1/2 tablespoon ground nutmeg
1/2 pound butter, melted

Note: You may substitute the crust of your choice.

2-1/4 pounds cream cheese at room temperature
4 eggs
1-1/2 teaspoons vanilla
1-1/2 cups sugar
1-1/2 tablespoons orange zest
2 cups pumpkin purée
3/4 pound white chocolate, chopped
2 tablespoons ground ginger
2 tablespoons ground allspice
1 tablespoon cinnamon

To make crust: Toast tortillas in 300 degree oven until crisp. Place tortillas and the sugar in a food processor and process until finely ground. Add cinnamon and process 30 seconds.

Place tortilla mixture in a large bowl. Add melted butter. Blend well with a fork or spatula until mixture is moistened. Place a generous amount into a 10" springform pan to cover bottom and make a 1/4" crust. Press mixture into pan to secure. Bake at 350 degrees until aromatic and toasty brown, approximately 45 minutes.

While crust is browning, place white chocolate in a food processor and pulse until granular.

Remove crusts from oven and divide white chocolate among each pan. Set aside.

Lower oven to 300 degrees.

To make cream cheese mixture: Whip cream cheese until softened. Add sugar and scrape down sides with spatula. Continue beating, adding eggs one at a time until well blended. Transfer mixture to a large bowl. Add vanilla, zest, pumpkin and all of the spices. Mix until well combined.

Pour into crust. Level off top. Lift and drop gently onto countertop to remove air bubbles. Place springform pan on a cookie sheet. Bake at 300 degrees for 45 minutes to an hour, until the top is lightly browned.

Remove and cool. When cool, gently open the springform pan and remove the cheesecake. Cover and chill 6 hours or overnight.

Too Easy Chocolate Mousse with Bourbon Caramel

Serves 4 to 6

Mousse
1-3/4 cups semi sweet chocolate chips
1 pint heavy whipping cream

Bourbon Caramel
1/2 cup sugar
1 cup heavy whipping cream
1 tablespoon bourbon

Place chocolate chips in a steel or glass mixing bowl. Put the mixing bowl on top of a pot of simmering water. Be sure the bowl creates a seal around the pot and be sure the water cannot touch the bowl. This could get the chocolate too hot and the bowl could break. While the chocolate is melting, whip the heavy cream in a mixing bowl with a whisk until it reaches soft peaks (if you touch the cream with your finger and lift it up, the cream should rise up a little, but not stand taller than 1 inch).

When the cream is whipped, the chocolate should be melted. Stir the chocolate with a rubber spatula until completely smooth.

With a rubber spatula, make a pool in the center of the whipped cream. Pour 1/3 of the melted chocolate into the center. Quickly stir about 15 tiny circles only where you poured the chocolate. Do not spread the chocolate throughout the cream. This will cause the chocolate to solidify in to chips in the cool cream. Add the remaining chocolate to the mixture, again only to the center. Continue to stir in the center until you have a smooth dark cream/chocolate mixture. Now, fold the center in to the rest of the bowl until smooth. Refrigerate for at least 2 hours.

Bourbon Caramel

In a saucepan, combine cream and bourbon. Bring to a boil. While this mixture is heating, heat sugar in another saucepan over medium high heat, stirring with a wooden spoon until it becomes a smooth bronze liquid. Remove from heat. Caution: this caramelized sugar is very hot. Do not let it touch your skin.

Add 1/3 of the cream mixture to the liquefied sugar, stirring fast when the bubbles die down. Add the remaining cream mixture, stirring until smooth.

Banana Caramel Cake

Serves 16 - 20

8 ounces butter, softened
3 cups sugar
4 eggs

4 cups banana, mashed
3/4 tablespoon baking soda
1-1/3 cups buttermilk

5 cups flour
1-1/2 tablespoons baking powder
dash salt
1 teaspoon cinnamon
1 cup pecans, chopped

Cream Cheese Icing
16 ounces cream cheese
4 ounces butter, softened
6 - 8 cups powdered sugar

Caramel Filling
2 cups caramels
3/4 cup heavy cream

Grease and flour two 10" cake pans.

Cream butter and sugar in the bowl of an electric mixer. Add the eggs. Mix for another couple of minutes until well blended.

Combine bananas, soda and buttermilk. Mix.

Alternately, add the dry ingredients and the banana mixture, starting with the dry ingredients, to prevent lumping. Mix completely, but do not overmix.

Pour into pans. Bake at 350 degrees for approximately 40 minutes. Remove from oven and let cool for 10 minutes. Run a knife around the sides of pan to loosen cake. Turn cake upside down onto plate. Cool completely.

Trim cake so it is flat on the top. Place cake on a platter or cake circle. Spread cake with about 1-1/2 cups of the cream cheese icing. Spread about 1/2 cup of the caramel on top of the cream cheese. Place the second cake layer on top of the caramel. Spread the remaining icing over the cake. Ladle more caramel on top of the cake so that it drizzles down the cake.

Serve as is or chill to set a little firmer.

Cream Cheese Icing
Cream cheese and butter together in the bowl of an electric mixer. Carefully add sugar a little at a time until you have the desired consistency. You may add a bit of milk or cream to thin the mixture, if necessary.

Caramel Filling
Heat caramels and cream together until thoroughly mixed. Cool.

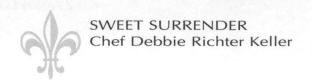
Flourless Truffle Torte

Serves 16

2 pounds semi sweet chocolate	Crème Anglaise
8 eggs, separated	*2 cups milk*
1 tablespoon flour	*6 egg yolks*
1 tablespoon sugar	*2/3 cup granulated sugar*
2 tablespoons water	

Grease, liberally flour and line a 10" round cake pan that is 2-1/2" high with parchment paper. Set aside.

Beat egg whites until stiff but not dry. Set aside. Melt chocolate and butter in a double boiler. Add egg yolks, flour, sugar and water. Mix well. Add egg whites to chocolate mixture. Fold together until completely blended. Pour mixture into prepared pan.

Bake at 350 degrees for 15 - 20 minutes. The torte will be firm around the outer part, but should still be a little soft on the inner area. Cool completely. Invert pan to remove torte.

Serve with Crème Anglaise.

Crème Anglaise
Whisk sugar and yolks together.

Heat 1-1/2 cups milk in a double boiler.

Add the remaining 1/2 cup of milk to the sugar and yolks mixture.

When the milk in the double boiler is warm to the touch, whisk it into the bowl with the milk/sugar/yolks mixture. Pour back into the double boiler and cook until it becomes thick enough that it coats the back of a spoon. If you were to blow on the coated spoon, the mixture would form a rose-like pattern or would petal out. When thickened, chill over an ice bath, or refrigerate to prevent further cooking.

SWEET SURRENDER
Chef Debbie Richter Keller

White Chocolate Mousse Torte with Oreo Cookie Crust

10 servings

Crust
24 Oreo cookies
1/4 cup (1/2 stick unsalted butter, melted)
3/4 cup whipping cream, chilled
8 ounces semisweet chocolate, chopped

Filling
16 ounces white chocolate, such as Lindt, chopped
3 cups whipping cream, chilled
1 tablespoon unflavored gelatin
1/4 cup water
1 teaspoon vanilla extract

Oreo cookies, chopped

To prepare crust: Grease a 10" diameter spring-form pan. Finely grind cookies in a food processor. Add melted butter and blend well. Press crust mix onto bottom of prepared pan.

In a heavy saucepan, simmer cream. Reduce heat to low. Add semisweet chocolate and whisk until melted and smooth. Pour chocolate mixture over crust. Chill

To prepare filling: Combine white chocolate and 1 cup of cream in the top of a double boiler. Heat over simmering water until chocolate is melted and smooth, stirring often. Remove top pan from over water. Set aside and cool to barely lukewarm.

Sprinkle gelatin over 1/4 cup water in heavy small saucepan. Let stand 10 minutes to soften. Stir over low heat until gelatin dissolves. Pour into a large bowl. Add remaining 2 cups cream and vanilla. Stir to combine. Beat cream/gelatin mixture to soft peaks. Fold in white chocolate mixture. Pour filling into crust. Refrigerate until filling is set, at least 6 hours. May be refrigerated overnight.

When ready to serve, run sharp knife around pan sides to loosen torte. Release sides of pan. Sprinkle with chopped cookies and serve.

Malted Coffee Ice Cream

Serves 8

2 cups milk
2 cups heavy cream
1/4 cup malt powder
6 egg yolks
1 cup sugar
3 ounces Mocha Java coffee beans
1/2 ounce Bourbon

Heat the coffee beans in the oven for 5 minutes at 325 degrees. Heat the cream, malt powder, milk and coffee beans together along with half of the sugar in a medium saucepan. Bring to a scald, and add the bourbon and allow the beans to steep for 5 more minutes. Then, blend in a blender or with a hand emulsifier until smooth. Mix the yolks with the remaining sugar and slowly add the hot mixture to the cold egg mixture until fully incorporated. Strain. Chill thoroughly and run the ice cream through an ice cream maker as directed by the manufacturer.

THE PALMER ROOM AT
LAKE FOREST COUNTRY CLUB
Chef Annette Saco

Heavenlies

Yield: About 3 dozen

1 stick Parkay
1 stick unsalted butter
1-1/4 cups sugar
1 cup flour, sifted
3 heaping tablespoons cocoa powder
1/2 teaspoon baking powder
1 cup walnuts, chopped
1 teaspoon vanilla

Filling
2 cups coconut
2 cans condensed milk

Frosting
3 tablespoons cocoa powder
3 tablespoons butter
1 teaspoon vanilla
1 pound powdered sugar, sifted
Milk, as needed to moisten

Mix all ingredients on low speed of a mixer. Press mixture onto a greased cookie sheet. Bake at 325 degrees for 20 minutes. Remove and let cool.

Filling

Mix together and let sit in the refrigerator for 20 minutes. Drop spoonfuls of filling on top of the crust. (Do not spread. Spreading will tear the crust). Bake at 325 degrees for 20 minutes or until golden brown. Remove from oven and immediately frost.

Frosting

Mix first four ingredients together until well blended. Add milk, if necessary. Apply frosting to cake. Spread carefully. Cut into 1" squares.

Buttermilk Panna Cotta with Quince and Apple Compote

Serves 6

1 tablespoon gelatin powder
1/4 cup cold water
2-1/2 cups buttermilk
1 cup sugar
2 cups sour cream
1 teaspoon vanilla extract

Quince and Apple Compote:
1/4 cup water
2 Granny Smith apples
2 quince
1 cinnamon stick
3/4 cup sugar

Nutmeg, to garnish
Whipped cream, to garnish
Cinnamon stick, to garnish

Dissolve gelatin in cold water. Let stand. Combine buttermilk, sugar, sour cream and vanilla, then bring to a simmer. Heat gelatin and water until just liquid, but do not boil. Whisk warm gelatin into warm buttermilk mixture and pour into six 4 ounce ramekins. Refrigerate until set, about 3 hours. To serve, remove panna cotta by running a knife around the edge of the ramekin and turn it upside down onto a plate to release.

Quince and Apple Compote
Peel and dice quince and apples. Place them in a saucepan with water, sugar and cinnamon stick. Cook on medium heat until the moisture has evaporated. Remove cinnamon stick and mash the fruit. Place a spoonful of the fruit mixture over the panna cotta or serve on the side. Garnish with nutmeg, whipped cream and a cinnamon stick.

Chocolate and Banana Dacquoise with Appleton Rum Anglaise

Serves 6

Meringue
3/4 cup almonds, finely ground
1-1/2 cups sugar
3/4 cup powdered sugar
4 large egg whites
1/2 teaspoon cream of tartar

Chocolate Ganache
12 ounces semisweet chocolate chips
(Callebaut preferably)
1-1/2 cups heavy cream

4 bananas

Appleton Rum Anglaise
1/2 cup sugar
4 egg yolks
1 cup milk
1/2 vanilla bean split or 1 teaspoon vanilla extract
1 ounce rum (Appleton rum preferred
but other rum may be used)

To prepare the meringue: Line a baking sheet with parchment paper. Draw 3 perfect circles of 7 inches in diameter for a template, then turn the paper over. In a food processor, add the nuts, cornstarch, and 1/2 the sugar and process until the texture is fine. In a mixer with a whisk attachment, mix the egg whites on medium speed until frothy. Add the cream of tartar and the remainder of the sugar and continue to whisk until stiff peaks form. Fold in the nut mixture. Immediately put in a pastry bag. Carefully and evenly, pipe onto the circles. Bake at 200 degrees for 1-1/2 to 2 hours, until dry but without any color.

While the meringue is cooling, prepare the ganache. Put the chocolate in a bowl. In a saucepan, bring the cream to a boil. Pour the cream over the chocolate and whisk until it is melted evenly. Distribute the ganache evenly over two of the meringue circles, leaving one plain. Slice the bananas and cover the two chocolate covered meringue pieces with the bananas. Stack the two discs, putting the plain disc on top. Dust the top with powdered sugar and refrigerate.

To prepare the anglaise: Whisk the yolks and sugar until it forms ribbons. In a saucepan with the milk, scrape the vanilla bean, and bring to a scald. Slowly whisk in the milk. Return the custard to the saucepan and on low heat stir continuously until it clings to the back of a spoon. Strain through a fine mesh strainer, add rum and cool completely.

For presentation: Ladle 1/4 cup of Anglaise in the center of a plate. Slice the dacquoise into 6 pieces and place each piece on top of the Anglaise and serve.

Crème Brûlée with Fresh Raspberries

Serves 7

10 egg yolks
4 cups heavy whipping cream
1 vanilla bean, split and scraped
1 cup sugar (2/3 for custard and 1/3 for the top of the desserts)
1 teaspoon almond extract
1 cup fresh raspberries

Preheat oven to 300 degrees. Combine cream, almond extract, the vanilla bean and the scrapings from the bean in a heavy sauce pan. Bring to a boil. Remove from heat and let steep for 15 minutes. In a medium bowl, whisk egg yolks and sugar until thickened. Stir hot cream mixture into yolks. Strain custard into seven 6 ounce ovenproof ramekins lined with fresh raspberries.

Put filled ramekins in a shallow baking dish and fill baking dish half way with water. Bake about 45 minutes or until set. Remove from oven. Chill for several hours.

To serve: Spread a thin, even layer of granulated sugar over the top of each crème brûlée. Carefully caramelize sugar with a small propane torch or in the broiler. Let sit until sugar hardens. Serve.

Hint: If broiling, put the brûlées as close to the heat source as possible.

VINCENZO'S
Chef Agostino Gabriele

Individual Chocolate Bombes

Serves 12

Base/Sponge Cake
5 eggs
3 egg yolks
3/4 cup sugar
1/2 teaspoon salt
1 1/4 cup flour

Soak for Cake
1 cup corn syrup
2 ounces Grand Marnier (optional)
2 ounces water

Chocolate Mousse
2 pounds semisweet chocolate
1 cup sugar
1 quart heavy cream

Frosting
1-1/4 pounds semisweet chocolate chips
2 cups cream

16 ounces white chocolate or nuts to decorate (optional)

Base/Sponge Cake
Mix eggs, egg yolk and salt until light and fluffy. Fold in flour. Pour into a 9" greased and floured cake pan. Bake at 350 degrees for 25 minutes, or until firm on top. Remove from oven and let sit about 10 minutes before removing from pan. Cut cake into three layers. Using any type of 2-1/2" cutter, cut into circles. Set aside.

Soak for Cake
Mix well and brush onto cake circles.

Chocolate Mousse
Melt chocolate in double boiler. In the bowl of a mixer, mix heavy cream with sugar until very soft peaks form. Add melted chocolate to cream a little at a time. Freeze.

Frosting
Melt semisweet chocolate in a double boiler. Add cream. Mix well. Let cool.

To assemble individual bombes: Using a #8 ice cream scoop, place a scoop of mousse on each cake circle. Spoon frosting over the mousse and cake until completely covered. Freeze until set.

Melt white chocolate in a double boiler. Let cool.

Remove cakes from freezer, let sit until a bit softer. Drizzle white chocolate over top of bombe (optional). Or, sprinkle with the nuts of your choice (optional). Serve.

Belgian Waffle De-Lite

Adjust for desired servings

Belgian waffle mix

Prepare the waffle mix as instructed on the package.

Top with:
*Godiva White Chocolate Raspberry
and Chocolate Truffle ice cream*

Split baby bananas in half and sprinkle with turbinado sugar. Then caramelize with a blow torch. Place bananas on top of the ice cream.

Add:
*Grilled fresh pineapple chopped
Seasonal berries
Chunks of mango*

Top with:
*Whipped cream sweetened with Coco Lopez
(a coconut flavored sweetener commonly used for piña coladas)
Toasted coconut
Chocolate sauce and Caramel sauce*

Note: The chocolate sauce and/or the caramel sauce can be flavored with bourbon or rum.

Chefs' Secrets

This is your chance to learn from the pros. Louisville's star chefs offer advice and share their secrets so that you can create culinary magic in your own kitchen.

What inspired you to become a chef?
I was always around kitchens when I was younger. My brother is a chef. I decided to work with him when I left school.

What kitchen tools do you recommend for the home cook?
The Japanese mandoline is great for slicing vegetables extra thin. • The Robot Coupe is excellent for making mousses, pasta and many other things. • Using a squeeze bottle for sauces and other types of presentation is a great way for the home cook to produce a restaurant style finish.

What kitchen utensil or tool do you not have but would like to receive as a gift?
I would be delighted if someone surprised me with a truffle slicer!

What is an important technique for the home cook to master?
Perfecting the knowledge to season things at precisely the right time.

Any humorous cooking anecdotes, either from your home or professional kitchen?
One evening, when I was working in Bermuda, I was serving venison. A guest asked me if it was local.

What are some common mistakes made by home cooks?
Working with dull knives. Sharpen your knives! • Not seasoning correctly. Pay careful attention to seasoning of a dish to bring out the flavors of each ingredient. • Getting all the dishes finished at the same time. I suggest working out a detailed timeline for the preparation of each dish.

If a snoopy neighbor were to look in your home refrigerator today, what would he find?
Not a lot. I eat out most nights. But, there's probably milk and cereal.

What's your favorite style of entertaining?
Al fresco. I really love dining outdoors.

If you're cooking for family or close friends, what is one of your favorite dishes to serve?
A large bowl of pasta, such as pappardelle with roasted tomatoes, pesto and fresh Parmesan, placed in the center of the table with plenty of fresh bread. Guests just help themselves.

If you were hosting an elegant dinner party, what would you serve?
Passed assorted canapés; foie gras terrine with Sauternes jelly; lobster consommé; a light salad; sorbet; lightly grilled John Dory; and apple tarte Tatin.

What are some of your favorite cookbooks?
El Bulli, by Feran Adria • *The French Laundry Cookbook*, by Thomas Keller

If you're going to indulge, what's your food of choice?
Háagen-Dazs ice cream!

What inspired you to become a chef?

I have a passion for cooking. Becoming a professional chef allowed me to be creative and to receive instant gratification in one profession.

What kitchen tools do you recommend for the home cook?

Chinese cleaver • Good quality blender • Food processor • Cutting board

What kitchen utensil or tool do you not have but would like to receive as a gift?

A warming/holding oven.

What are the most important techniques for the home cook to master?

Timing • Knife skills

What is one of the most common mistakes made by home cooks?

Not having all the ingredients to prepare the planned meal.

If a snoopy neighbor were to look in your home refrigerator today, what would he find?

Quite a few bottles of sauce and several sundried products – tomatoes, scallops, oysters and baby shrimp.

What's your favorite style of entertaining?

I prefer sit-down dinners because they enable the guests to converse and really enjoy each others' company. That type of dinner is also idea for relaxing and savoring the food.

If you're cooking for family or close friends, what are some of your favorite dishes to serve?

Beef Rendang – Malaysian style simmered curry beef; and Malaysian style noodle dishes. I love noodles. I could eat them all day long.

If you were hosting an elegant dinner party, what would you serve?

I would have an eclectic global menu featuring creative dishes that represent the best of several cuisines.

If you're going to indulge, what's your food of choice?

Whatever is fresh and good at the time, wherever I am.

Any final advice for the home cook?

Don't be picky about food you aren't knowledgeable about. Try a little of everything. Be innovative when you're planning your menus. Expose your friends and family to new tastes and new dishes.

What inspired you to become a chef?

I started my culinary journey when I was eight years old. I wanted pie, and I was going to have it. So, I baked one using peaches that my mom had canned during the summer. Following a Betty Crocker recipe for easy pie crust, I created my first masterpiece. It didn't taste too bad, either.

Because my mom worked the graveyard shift for most of my teenage years, I was responsible for preparing the evening meal. That is when I honed my casserole skills. When I wasn't cooking dinner, my mom introduced my sister and me to interesting foods such as Japanese soba noodles with beef, chile rellenos, and braised beef heart with egg noodles.

After leaving the house at the age of 18, I worked in a professional kitchen. I started out as a dish dog, an affectionate name for a dishwasher, who occasionally moonlighted as a line cook. I worked my way up to a lead line cook before deciding to follow a girl to Louisville where I enrolled in Sullivan College.

I soon started my tour at the English Grill under Chef Joe Castro. Salads and cold appetizers were my first stations, but I quickly made my way through them all, with my favorite being the sauce station. I loved the fast pace, the finesse and the creative opportunity. It wasn't long before I was promoted to sous chef.

After taking a 2200 mile backpacking trip from Georgia to Maine, I returned to Washington only to learn about a job in Louisville, my former home. Now, here I am at Avalon.

What kitchen tools do you recommend for the home cook?

Wooden spoons • Cast iron cookware, including a cast iron Dutch oven for roasts • Sharp knives (they don't have to be super expensive but they absolutely have to be sharp!) • A Japanese mandoline for fine cuts.

What kitchen utensil or tool do you not have but would like to receive as a gift?

A full set of All-Clad cookware would be a welcome surprise.

What is one of the most important techniques for the home cook to master?

Braising is a lost art and needs to be rediscovered by the home cook. When a meat or vegetable is properly braised, it can be a truly wonderful thing.

Any humorous cooking anecdotes, either from your home or professional kitchen?

I've been burning a lot of my home meals lately. We just had our first child, a girl. I will walk away from what's cooking and snuggle with her and my wife and forget about what's in the oven or on the stove.

What is a common mistake made by home cooks?

The biggest problem is usually putting too much food into one pan while you're trying to sauté. When a pan is too full, you're no longer sautéing; you're essentially steaming the ingredients.

If a snoopy neighbor were to look in your home refrigerator today, what would he find?

Olives, good Parmesan, beer, frozen pizza, potstickers, and old leftovers.

What's your favorite style of entertaining?

I like potluck-style get-togethers. Not only do I have to work a little less, but it's fun to taste everybody's favorite food.

If you're cooking for family or close friends, what is one of your favorite dishes to serve?

Pork butt that has been brined overnight in salt water and garlic, then rubbed with cumin, coriander and black pepper, then roasted with root vegetables.

If you were hosting an elegant dinner party, what would you serve?

I host an elegant dinner party six nights a week!

What are some of your favorite cookbooks?

Chez Panise Vegetables, by Alice Waters • *Sauces: Classic and Contemporary Sauce Making,* by James Peterson • *Larousse Gastronomique.*

If you're going to indulge, what's your food of choice?

Sushi, and lots of it. Or is it foie gras? I can't decide.

**BOB BORGERDING,
CHEF DE CUISINE
Azalea Restaurant**

What inspired you to become a chef?
A friend of my father became a mentor to me. I began my culinary career working with him in his restaurant.

What kitchen tools do you recommend for the home cook?
An immersion blender is great for making sauces and milk shakes. • A chef's knife and a paring knife are essential. I recommend Global knives because of their perfect balance. • A piping bag with an assortment of piping tips will help you present your dishes like a pro.

What kitchen utensil or tool do you not have but would like to receive as a gift?
There are several that come to mind. But, if I had to choose one, I'd say a fresh pasta roller.

What are the most important techniques for the home cook to master?
The basics! Grilling, sautéing, broiling, poaching and baking. • Here's a handy tip: when working with avocados, always keep the flesh near the pit. This helps prevent the flesh from turning brown.

What is one of the most common mistakes made by home cooks?
Home cooks are often afraid of straying from the recipe. You need to look at a recipe as a guideline. Also, realize that you can sometimes alter the dish and even make it better by the addition or deletion of one ingredient.

If a snoopy neighbor were to look in your home refrigerator today, what would he find?
Deli meat... a lot of deli meats. • Fajitas fixings.

What's your favorite style of entertaining?
Outdoor barbecues. Everything is improvised. There's no real script. Almost all foods can be barbecued. Once the aroma of the grill hits your nose, you just have to call some friends to enjoy it.

If you're cooking for family or close friends, what is one of your favorite dishes to serve?
For my large family, I like to serve a pan of lasagna, or some other baked pasta dish.

If you were hosting an elegant dinner party, what would you serve?
Elegant and fancy food such as caviar, foie gras, lobster and fresh truffles!

What are some of your favorite cookbooks?
The Professional Chef, by The Culinary Institute of America • *The Kitchen Sessions with Charlie Trotter.*

If you're going to indulge, what's your food of choice?
Fresh ceviche – tuna or good snapper.

Do you have any tips for controlling food costs at home?
Buy fresh • Buy seasonal.

Any final advice for the home cook?
Never be afraid of cooking any type of food. • Think of a recipe only as a guideline. Use your creativity to make adjustments. • Baking is a science. • Think outside the box.

What inspired you to become a chef?

Working closely with chefs in some of Louisville's best restaurants inspired me to learn the trade. I started in the business as a dishwasher in 1983 at Café Metro. I came up through the ranks while working with some of the great cooks of the time, such as Jim Henry, Rick Torres and Michael Driskell, to name just a few.

What kitchen tools do you recommend for the home cook?

Good wooden spoons • Stainless steel spoons • Several sets of tongs • Food processor • An array of high quality, sharp knives • *The Joy of Cooking* cookbook.

What kitchen utensil or tool do you not have but would like to receive as a gift?

A good juice-making machine would be a great gift for me, if anyone is asking.

What are the most important techniques for the home cook to master?

A home cook should cook with love. Cultivate a relationship with your kitchen tools and foods that you like to work with. • Being able to read and follow recipes is a huge plus.

What are some of the most common mistakes made by home cooks?

Too many people are intimidated in the kitchen. If you can read, you can cook! • Many cooks try to make dishes too complicated. Keep it simple! The best meals are usually the simplest ones. • Make sure you have ALL of the ingredients, and the freshest possible BEORE you begin a recipe. • Experiment.

Do you have any humorous anecdotes from either your professional or home kitchen?

Well, there was a time when a fellow line cook thought he was a chicken. He just lost it during a busy shift. We had to restrain him until the ambulance arrived.

If a snoopy neighbor were to look in your home refrigerator today, what would he find?

Organic salad dressing • Spinach • Rice milk • Spring water • Micro nutrient drinks.

What's your favorite style of entertaining?

I like to have sit-down dinners where everyone passes the food around the table family style. Whether it is a business dinner or one with family and friends, passing bowls of food is an intimate and soulful experience.

If you're cooking for family or close friends, what are some of your favorite dishes to serve?

I try not to cook for friends! I would rather order in pizza, or better yet, go to someone else's restaurant and let them cook for me!

If you were hosting an elegant dinner party, what would you serve?

I love pasta. I would probably toss some tortellini or penne with seasonal vegetables, olive oil, garlic, white wine and just a touch of butter. Throw in a spring mix salad with balsamic vinaigrette with feta. Add some good wine and hardy bread and you have a simple, elegant, flavorful dinner.

What are some of your favorite cookbooks?

Every kitchen should have a copy of *The Joy of Cooking*, by Erma S. Rombauer and Marion Rombauer Becker. • *The New Basics*, by Julie Rosso and Sheila Lukins is a great all-around cookbook.

If you're going to indulge, what's your food of choice?

A Super Sized Double Quarter Pounder Meal from McDonald's.

Do you have any tips for controlling food costs at home?

Start with learning the proper portion size for the people you are serving. Most people prepare way too much food!

Any final advice for the home cook?

Use recipes as a starting point. Most of them are tried and true, but that doesn't mean that they can't be improved upon. • Cook for fun. Don't get stressed out over serving the "perfect" meal. Most people appreciate an invitation and the effort that goes into planning a meal. They are not expecting perfection. • Cook with your heart.

What inspired you to become a chef?

As a kid, I wanted to be a truck driver or a chef. My mother was a great cook. Her influence made me decide to choose the culinary field.

What kitchen tools do you recommend for the home cook?

Whisks of various sizes • Food processor • Heavy bottom pots and pans of different sizes • German brand chef's and paring knives • Plastic cutting board.

What kitchen tool do you not have but would like to receive as a gift?

A food processor.

What are the most important techniques for the home cook to master?

Proper use of knives (and knowledge of the various cuts) • Understanding cooking temperatures • Good sanitary procedures.

Do you have any humorous anecdotes, either from your home or professional kitchen?

In 1983, during a Sunday brunch, a customer asked me what entrée I was serving. "Rabbit," I replied. She became very upset and started screaming in the dining room that I was very insensitive to not think about children. That particular Sunday was Easter!

What are some of the most common mistakes made by home cooks?

Not reading through recipes • Not having all ingredients ready (mise en place) • Over-cooking steaks.

If a snoopy neighbor were to look in your home refrigerator today, what would he find?

Beer, of course! Butter, cream, eggs, cheeses and fresh vegetables.

What is your favorite style of entertaining?

Buffets, so I can sit down and enjoy the meal, too.

If you're cooking for family or close friends, what are some of your favorite dishes to serve?

Fresh mussels cooked with leeks, carrots, celery and white wine, served with French fries • Venison • Steak.

If you were hosting an elegant dinner party, what would you serve?

Cold appetizer: A nice paté (duck with Grand Marnier).

Soup: Either a lobster bisque or a beef consommé

Salad: Avocado and pear with creamy balsamic vinaigrette.

Intermezzo: Lime sorbet.

Hot appetizer: Sea scallops with roasted red bell pepper sauce.

Entrée: Beef Wellington with fresh vegetable medley and a potato croquette.

Dessert: White chocolate with raspberry sauce in a chocolate tulip.

Coffee and After Dinner drinks.

What are some of your favorite cookbooks?

The Joy of Cooking • *Recettes de la Pyramide*, by Fernand Point • It's not a cookbook, but I really like Bon Appétit magazine.

If you're going to indulge, what's your food of choice?

Butter.

Do you have any tips for controlling food costs at home?

Use newspaper or mail coupons. • Don't throw away leftovers.

Any final advice for the home cook?

If you have any problems or questions, call me!
• Use fresh ingredients whenever possible.
• Cooking is an art and art needs patience.

What inspired you to become a chef?
My mother and Graham Kerr's television show.

What kitchen tools do you recommend for the home cook?
A lemon juicer because fresh juice in any dish is better than bottled. • A zester because the oil in the fruit's peel adds extra flavor • A blender because it is great for drinks, as well as for purées.

What kitchen utensil or tool do you not have but would like to receive as a gift?
A Weber grill • Krup's Panini Press.

What are the most important techniques for the home cook to master?
I recommend that home cooks work on perfecting their baking skills, and the art of pastry making and sauce making.

Do you have any general advice for the home cook?
Be sure to give yourself enough time in the kitchen so you don't have to rush your preparation. • Clean up as you work. • Take time to enjoy what you cook!

If a snoopy neighbor were to look in your home refrigerator today, what would he find?
Potato salad • Deli meats • Chitterlings • Macaroni and cheese • Cole slaw • Kale greens • Meat loaf with mushroom demi glace • Mixed vegetables • Kool Aid • Chocolate milk • Orange juice • Whole wheat bread • Mayonnaise.

What's your favorite style of entertaining?
Buffets.

If you're cooking for family or close friends, what are some of your favorite dishes to serve?
Shrimp cocktail, salads, lasagna, baked ziti with meatballs, barbecue chicken, grilled flank steak, grilled chicken with rosemary, pound cake with strawberries, and iced tea.

If you were hosting an elegant dinner party, what would you serve?
Assorted appetizers; roast duck salad with blood orange vinaigrette; grilled lobster with basil butter; tenderloin of beef with brie and spinach; and a flourless chocolate cake with ice cream.

What are some of your favorite cookbooks?
The Dean and Deluca Cookbook • *The Joy of Cooking*, by Irma S. Rombauer • *The Professional Chef*, by The Culinary Institute of America • *Eat More, Weigh Less*, by Dr. Dean Ornish • *The Betty Crocker Cookbook*.

If you're going to indulge, what are your foods of choice?
Caviar, smoked fish, pasta, assorted beef dishes, shellfish, vegetables, and all sweets.

Any final advice for the home cook?
Watch food shows on television • Buy cookbooks • Have more parties.

What inspired you to become a chef?

Being a commercial art major, I never attended culinary school. I had an eye for food and design. Cooking just came naturally to me. It helped growing up in a family in which everyone was a wonderful cook and everyone loved food. For me, cooking is a passion. I take great pride in it. I love to see the smiles on people's faces when they can't put down their fork.

What kitchen tools do you recommend for the home cook?

I think every home chef needs a large cutting board and plenty of work space. • To prepare nice food, you don't need all of the utensils that are marketed today. But, four knives are essential: chef's, paring, serrated and utility.

What kitchen utensil or tool do you not have but would like to receive as a gift?

I'm actually thinking of more than kitchen utensils! For starters, I'd like an outdoor kitchen. Other than that, probably a couple of wall ovens for more space when I have parties. I'd also like just a little more counter space. I've got the rest covered.

What is one of the most important techniques for the home cook to master?

Proper knife skills are critical to preparing multi course meals and simple everyday food preparation. Good knife skills and a little creativity go a long way.

What are some common mistakes made by home cooks?

Timing is everything when preparing meals. Remember to keep an eye on everything. Using a timer really helps. • Remember, you don't have to follow the recipe exactly. Think of the recipe as a concept. • Have every bit of your "prep" completed before you begin cooking. • And, clean up as you cook!

If a snoopy neighbor were to look in your home refrigerator today, what would he find?

Milk, fresh fruit, cheese, Gatorade, fresh vegetables, butter and yogurt. Oh, and pudding and ice cream for my daughter.

What's your favorite style of entertaining?

I enjoy sit-down dinners because you get to interact and speak more intimately with everyone. Also, you get to watch everyone enjoy your food. I also like barbecues because the weather is usually beautiful, the food is great and everyone is relaxed. And, if you drop sauce on your shirt, not everyone notices.

If you're cooking for family or close friends, what are some of your favorite dishes to serve?

You can't go wrong with some sort of meat, such as a ribeye steak, veal chop or pork chop, that is just grilled or pan seared with salt and pepper and a dab of butter on top. Sometimes I go all out with five courses. I really don't have a favorite dish to serve. I love to cook everything.

If you were hosting an elegant dinner party, what would you serve?

I would have foie gras; wild mushroom risotto with shaved truffles; cold asparagus soup with quail egg and caviar; pan seared duck breast with sherry fig sauce, served with whipped parsnips and asparagus; a fine selection of cheeses; and a chocolate dessert.

What are some of your favorite cookbooks?

My grandmother's and mother's recipes are my favorite resources. But, two great guides to cooking are *Larousse Gastronomique* and *Mastering the Art of French Cooking*, by Julia Child.

If you're going to indulge, what are your foods of choice?

Foie gras, barbecue, French cheeses and ice cream.

Any final advice for the home cook?

The most important thing in cooking is to use fresh, quality meats, fish and produce. Fresh produce is essential. It makes all the difference. • If you have time, learn to make your own stocks and learn how to clean a whole fish. • Also, try to cook a meal without opening up any cans! • Enjoy what you do. • Be creative and don't be afraid to try something new.

What inspired you to become a chef?

I've always enjoyed food, but didn't really become seriously interested in cooking until I was in college. After wandering aimlessly through four different majors over the course of my time at university, I realized that what I really wanted to do for a living was to be a cook. Since then, I've been lucky enough to work for and with some really amazing cooks and chefs. I've learned from, and been inspired by, all of them.

What kitchen tools do you recommend for the home cook?

Two of the most useful tools in any home kitchen are a good quality chef's knife and a good paring knife. • With good knives and enough workspace to use them, you can do a lot of great food. • Also, I recommend a full size professional style cutting board. Those tiny cutting boards made for home use don't give you any room to work.

What kitchen utensil or tool do you not have but would like to receive as a gift?

A restaurant grade immersion blender. Home models are nice, but it's like the difference between driving a Civic and a Humvee. They'll both get you where you want to go, but with the restaurant grade professional model you'll be able to take shortcuts, get there faster and have a lot more fun doing it.

What is one of the most important techniques for the home cook to master?

Learning when and how to season foods. It's generally better to season foods before and during the cooking process rather than after. Food cooked along with the proper amount of salt and pepper is always going to taste better than food that has had seasonings added after cooking.

Any humorous cooking anecdotes, either from your home or professional kitchen?

Yes, but none of them are fit for publication.

What is one of the most common mistakes made by home cooks?

Avoiding salt and fat to the point of making food tasteless. Salt and fat are a cook's best friends. More often than not, when a dish doesn't taste quite as good as it should, a little more salt or a little butter will fix it right up.

If a snoopy neighbor were to look in your home refrigerator today, what would he find?

Ale-8-1 soft drinks, carry out pizza from Pizzeria Due in Chicago, Best's Kosher Hot Dogs, and eleven different types of mustard. I really like mustard.

What's your favorite style of entertaining?

I guess I would have to say that having people over for a cook-out is my favorite way of entertaining. With as much time as I spend cooking at work, I like to keep cooking at home as simple as possible. It doesn't get much simpler than building a fire, throwing some good steaks on and making a couple of nice side dishes.

If you're cooking for family or close friends, what are some of your favorite dishes to serve?

I like to do simple, hearty one pot dishes at home. Lots of pot roast and chili. Also, during warm weather, I really enjoying cooking outdoors over a live fire. Everything tastes better when cooked over a wood fire.

If you were hosting an elegant dinner party, what would you serve?

I just can't see myself hosting anything more elegant than a barbecue.

What are some of your favorite cookbooks?

Jasper White's Cooking From New England • *Chef Prudhomme's Louisiana Kitchen,* by Paul Prudhomme • *Cooking with Patrick Clark* • *Cucina Simpatica,* by Johanne Killeen • *James Beard's Theory and Practice of Good Cooking* • *Great American Food,* by Charlie Palmer • *The Lutece Cookbook,* by André Soltner

If you're going to indulge, what's your food of choice?

Graeter's chocolate chip ice cream.

BEA CHAMBERLAIN,
CHEF/OWNER
El Mundo

What inspired you to become a chef?

Having to work my way through college, I cooked, waited tables, served drinks, washed dishes, and fell in love with the restaurant business. The cooking part came naturally and I pursued that aspect of the business after college and went to culinary art school. It's such a crazy business. You have to love it to actually do it.

What kitchen tools do you recommend for the home cook?

One of the most important things a home cook needs is larger than a traditional kitchen tool. You need a gas stove in order to control heat well. Plus, you can do all kinds of things with the flame, such as roast peppers. • I like the Cuisinart food processor for its diversity. • And, I definitely suggest one high carbon stainless steel knife that you can easily keep sharp with a stone.

What kitchen utensil or tool do you not have but would like to receive as a gift?

A pasta machine.

What are the most important techniques for the home cook to master?

Knife Skills 101 • Patience.

What are home cooks' most common mistakes?

Overcooking meat and fish. • Not cleaning as you go. • Not using fresh herbs. Grow an herb garden!

If a snoopy neighbor were to look in your home refrigerator today, what would he find?

I shop when I want to cook something, so my refrigerator is now full of garlic, chile paste, ketchup, rooster sauce, Asian fish sauce, pickled jalapeños, goat cheese, white wine, ginger, carrots, To-go boxes and vitamins.

What's your favorite style of entertaining?

Casual, one-pot dishes enjoyed with friends.

If you're cooking for family or close friends, what is one of your favorite dishes to serve?

Lasagna with spinach and mushrooms.

If you were hosting an elegant dinner party, what would you serve?

Asian-style lobster, stir-fried with ginger, garlic, green onion, cilantro, soy sauce, white wine and lemongrass.

What are some of your favorite cookbooks?

The Art of Mexican Cooking, by Diana Kennedy • *The Fine Art of Italian Cooking*, by Giuliano Bugialli • *The Simple Art of Vietnamese Cooking*, by Binh Duong • *The Babbo Cookbook*, by Mario Bitali • *Stalking the Blue-eyed Scallop*, by Euell Gibbons.

If you're going to indulge, what are your foods of choice?

Crown roast of pork • Potato chips • Lobster.

Tips for controlling food costs at home:

Buy ingredients that you can use in lots of different dishes.

Any final advice for the home cook?

Keep on cookin.'

114   SECRETS OF LOUISVILLE CHEFS

What inspired you to become a chef?
My mother and father inspired me. It's what I love to do.

What kitchen tools do you recommend for the home cook?
A large chef's knife (10" - 12") • Silpat mat • Heavy cookware • Cast iron skillet

What kitchen utensil or tool do you not have but would like to receive as a gift?
A good diamond knife sharpener.

What are some of the most important techniques for the home cook to master?
Patience • Proper seasoning, especially salt and pepper • Start with a hot skillet

What are home cooks' most common mistakes?
Not waiting for the cookware to reach the correct temperature on the range • Forgetting the salt and pepper.

What's your favorite style of entertaining?
It varies with the seasons and with the friends I invite.

If you're cooking for family or close friends, what are some of your favorite dishes to serve?
I tend to lean towards one pot -- comfort foods, foods that have memories built in.

If you were hosting an elegant dinner party, what would you serve?
Salad of Peking Duck Spring Roll; Chili Gastrique and Miso and Carrot Vinaigrette; Roasted Loin of Lamb with Spinach and White Truffle Gnocchi, Natural Lamb jus and Italian parsley; Apple Beignets with Bourbon Sabayon. All dishes would be matched with great beverages.

What is one of your favorite cookbooks?
Southern Food, by John Egerton

If you're going to indulge, what's your food of choice?
Fresh seafood

Any final advice for the home cook?
Relax. Cooking is therapeutic. Let your senses go wild.

What inspired you to become a chef?
Having the opportunity to work with so many great chefs as a young apprentice, and the energy and excitement of a four star kitchen.

What kitchen tools do you recommend for the home cook?
8" chef's knife • Cuisinart food processor • Mandoline • All-Clad cookware • Vita Mix blender • KitchenAid mixer

What kitchen utensil or tool do you not have but would like to receive as a gift?
An electric pasta machine.

What are the most important techniques for the home cook to master?
The art of proper sautéing • The art of deglazing • Basic knife skills for consistent cuts • Patience and perseverance • Organization.

Any humorous anecdotes, either from your home or professional kitchen?
I was once invited to a house for dinner and was promptly taken into the kitchen by the host. He opened the refrigerator and said, "Now what can you do with this stuff?"

What are home cooks' most common mistakes?
No patience • To measure incorrectly • Not adjusting the flavoring as the dish nears completion. • Lack of organization • Lack of proper mise en place (having all ingredients prepared before beginning the recipe)

If a snoopy neighbor were to look in your home refrigerator today, what would he find?
More than 25 hot sauces, pickles and mustards, various relishes and salsas, plenty of cheese, Fiji artisinal water, and Kaliber non-alcoholic beer.

What's your favorite style of entertaining?
I prefer a multi course sit-down dinner with a variety of personalities present. Great food, great wine and great conversation.

If you're cooking for family or close friends, what are some of your favorite dishes to serve?
Lasagna • Pork Adobo • Pot Roast.

If you were hosting an elegant dinner party, what would you serve?
Tasting portions of multiple courses.

What are some of your favorite cookbooks?
The New Texas Cuisine, by Stephen Pyles • *The Babbo Cookbook*, by Mario Batali • Any of Charlie Trotter's cookbooks • *The Joy of Cooking* • And, a great reference book, *Visual Food Encyclopedia*.

If you're going to indulge, what are your foods of choice?
Dim Sum • Any dumpling • Prime beef • South African Lobster brandade

Do you have any tips for controlling food costs at home?
Buy what you need for the recipe. Any leftovers can be incorporated into soup or stock for the future.

Any final advice for the home cook?
Don't be afraid of new ingredients • Experiment often • Take chances • Overcome mistakes • Make time to enjoy the romance and fun of food.

What inspired you to become a chef?

I have loved to cook since I was 17 years old growing up in Ierapetra, Greece. I began cooking for family and friends for holiday gatherings. I moved to the United States in 1997 with the goal of opening my own restaurant. In 2000, I opened the Greek Paradise Café in Radcliff, Kentucky. Then, in 2002, I opened the Greek Paradise Café in Louisville. I have the pleasure of serving my native cuisine everyday. It's like inviting guests into my own home to savor Greek food and hospitality.

What kitchen tools do you recommend for the home cook?

If you don't have great knives, it's impossible to prep well. The chef's knife, paring knife and peeler are absolutely essential for me. • I also recommend several different size whisks for making gravies and sauces and a meat thermometer so you don't over-cook meat. • Of course, you can't have too many spatulas and ladles. • Other tools I can't cook without are my food processor, grill pan, mandoline, and mortar and pestle.

What kitchen utensil or tool do you not have but would like to receive as a gift?

A complete set of Wüsthof knives.

Any humorous cooking anecdotes, either from your home or professional kitchen?

I once set fire to my restaurant kitchen while demonstrating to a guest how to flambé. No one was ever in danger because we immediately put out the fire. I don't want to discourage people from flambéing, but be sure to have a fire extinguisher handy!

What are some of the most common mistakes made by home cooks?

Home cooks often get discouraged because they don't have all the ingredients for a recipe on hand. • Also, they don't prepare each ingredient before beginning the recipe.

If a snoopy neighbor were to look in your home refrigerator today, what would he find?

Lots of fruits, vegetables and cheese. My refrigerator looks like a farmer's market. If you don't have any meat, or if you prefer not to use meat, you can whip up great entrées with only vegetables and cheese. What will you not find in my refrigerator? Leftovers. I try to prepare everything fresh for each meal. But, my refrigerator is so well stocked that no one can complain that there isn't anything to eat in my house.

What's your favorite style of entertaining?

I like to host buffets because I can let my imagination run wild when I'm planning the menu. Usually, I can prepare many of the dishes in advance. And, buffets lend themselves to a beautiful display.

If you're cooking for family or close friends, what are some of your favorite dishes to serve?

Leg of lamb with fresh thyme, rosemary and garlic. I have an herb garden so it's easy to step outside for wonderful herbs. I cook the lamb in its own juices until it falls off the bone. I serve it with oven roasted potatoes. A heavenly combination. It's what my friends request when I invite them to dinner. I always want to serve something different, but they protest so much that I end up serving the lamb and potatoes once again.

If you're going to indulge, what's your food of choice?

Salmon kabobs and Kritikos, a Greek red wine. I sit in front of the television, watch *Sex in the City*, and forget all my troubles.

What are some tips for controlling food costs?

Stay away from frozen foods. They may be tempting because they're convenient, but they're also expensive and not nearly as good as food you prepare yourself. • Always watch for sales and clip coupons. I'm a big coupon clipper. But, for price and quality, you can't beat a farmer's market.

Any final advice for the home cook?

You need to love yourself, so cook healthy and delicious dishes. • Experimen... don't be afraid to try new dishes. • The best advice? Cook Greek!

What inspired you to become a chef?
I like to produce things that give people satisfaction, pleasure and enjoyment. Being a chef is never dull. There's always a new technique or an ingredient to try.

What kitchen tools do you recommend for the home cook?
A good French knife • Heavy bottom pans • A slotted fish spatula • A gas stove.

What kitchen utensil or tool do you not have but would like to receive as a gift?
An immersion blender would be at home in my kitchen.

What are the most important techniques for the home cook to master?
It may sound like a lot to learn, but you can have fun learning each technique. So, I'd suggest the basics. • Proper searing • Roasting • Sautéing • Braising • Frying

If a snoopy neighbor were to look in your home refrigerator today, what would he find?
I always have a chicken in the refrigerator. Keeping it company are plenty of fresh vegetables and bottled water.

What are some of the most common mistakes made by home cooks?
Not being prepared. • Not taking the time to do things properly.

What's your favorite style of entertaining?
I prefer sit-down dinners simply because I feel more comfortable doing this style.

If you're cooking for family or close friends, what is one of your favorite dishes to serve?
Coq au Vin. That's why I always have a chicken in the refrigerator.

If you were hosting an elegant dinner party, what would you serve?
Foie gras and seared veal.

What is your favorite cookbook?
Ducasse Flavors of France, by Alain Ducasse.

If you're going to indulge, what's your food of choice?
Lamb chops.

Do you have any tips for controlling food costs at home?
Utilize leftovers for lunch and light snacks.

Any final advice for the home cook?
Always give yourself adequate time. • Always buy local and fresh products as often as possible.

What inspired you to become a chef?
My mom was a great cook, so I was exposed to lots of flavors as a kid. When I saw the art in it, I was turned on from the start.

What kitchen tools do you recommend for the home cook?
An immersion blender for soups and purees • A cast iron skillet. Everyone should have one.

What kitchen utensil or tool do you not have but would like to receive as a gift?
A mini food processor.

What are the most important techniques for the home cook to master?
Cooking times and temperatures.

What is one of the most common mistakes made by home cooks?
Not having everything finished at the same time, and at the right temperature. I suggest that the home cook work out a time table for preparation and for cooking.

If a snoopy neighbor were to look in your home refrigerator today, what would he find?
Lots of cheese. I love cheese. And some red wine, too!

If you're cooking for family or close friends, what are some of your favorite dishes to serve?
Cocktail food, or tapas, so the guests can grab what they want. They get a chance to taste several different things.

If you were hosting an elegant dinner party, what would you serve?
Ceviches, a kind of "seafood salsa," are a great way to start. I'd also serve some grilled meats with Chimichurri.

What are some of your favorite cookbooks?
Latin Ladles, by Douglas Rodriguez • Alan Wong's Asian cookbooks.

If you're going to indulge, what's your food of choice?
Foie gras. I love it with berries and cheese or mushrooms and Dijon. It's wonderful!

Do you have any tips for controlling food costs at home?
Utilize leftovers in other dishes.

Any final advice for the home cook?
Use timers • Don't be afraid of failure. That's the best way to learn.

DANIEL STAGE,
CHEF
Le Relais

What kitchen tools do you recommend for the home cook?

Chinois • Chinese cap sieve, a fine conical strainer • A good chef's knife • Piano wire whip • 6 qt. KitchenAid mixer • Heavy bottom pans.

What kitchen utensil or tool do you not have but would like to receive as a gift?

I'm lucky to have almost everything!

What are the most important techniques for the home cook to master?

You need to have a basic understanding of all techniques because in cooking you need to use different ones to give a dish texture and depth.

What are some common mistakes made by home cooks?

They don't have a grasp of the basics of cooking, yet they try to cook with ingredients using products and techniques they don't understand. I suggest they buy some cookbooks on basic techniques.

If a snoopy neighbor were to look in your home refrigerator today, what would he find?

Not too much. I usually go to the market and try to buy fresh ingredients that I will use that day.

What's your favorite style of entertaining?
Sit-down dinners.

If you're cooking for family or close friends, what are some of your favorite dishes to serve?
I really don't know. We would probably sit around and talk about what sounds good and then go to the market and just start buying things.

If you were hosting an elegant dinner party, what would you serve?
Foie gras, consommé, wild mushrooms, lamb and tuna.

What are some of your favorite cookbooks?
Larousse Gastronomique • *Le Cordon Bleu Complete Cooking Techniques.*

If you're going to indulge, what are your foods of choice?
Wild mushrooms • Cheese • Foie gras • Quail.

What inspired you to become a chef?

The wonderful, warm and talented African American woman who cooked in my mother's and grandmother' kitchens.

What kitchen tools do you recommend for the home cook?

KitchenAid mixer • Vita Mix blender • Cuisinart food processor.

What kitchen utensil or tool do you not have but would like to receive as a gift?

A new, bigger Viking stove!

What is one of the most important techniques for the home cook to master?

Sauce making. Because it is one of the hardest things to do right.

What is one of the most common mistakes made by home cooks?

Being intimidated by recipes – a terrible curse.

If a snoopy neighbor were to look in your home refrigerator today, what would he find?

Orange juice, milk, cheese, capers, mustard, mayonnaise, organic eggs, bagels, Plugra butter, and always, apples.

What's your favorite style of entertaining?

Sit down dinners and the fun of presentation: the "Ah!" of entertaining!

If you're cooking for family or close friends, what are some of your favorite dishes to serve?

Lamb shanks, mussels in the outdoor oven, homemade bread, large salads and fruit galettes.

What are some of your favorite cookbooks?

Soups of France, by Lois Rothert • *From Earth to Table,* by John Ash • *The French Laundry Cookbook,* by Thomas Keller • *Amuse-Bouche,* by Rick Tramonto

If you're going to indulge, what's your food of choice?

Foie gras.

Do you have any tips for controlling food costs at home?

Go to small grocery stores, with a list for just a few days.

Any final advice for the home cook?

Believe in leftovers!

What inspired you to become a chef?
Helping my mom in the kitchen. And, I get satisfaction seeing people enjoying my creations.

What kitchen tools do you recommend for the home cook?
I recommend basic tools, especially any tool that will lend itself to more than one use.

What kitchen utensil or tool do you not have but would like to receive as a gift?
A pressure cooker.

What are the most important techniques for the home cook to master?
Frying • Braising • Sautéing • Poaching • Roasting and baking.

Any humorous anecdotes, either from your home or professional kitchen?
Everyday is fun and interesting

What are some common mistakes made by home cooks?
Not reading the recipe before getting started. • Not having all the ingredients and tools ready.

If a snoopy neighbor were to look in your home refrigerator today, what would he find?
Nothing but frozen pizza.

What's your favorite style of entertaining?
Sit-down dinners. I like to wow people with my creations.

If you're cooking for family or close friends, what is one of your favorite dishes to serve?
Any chicken dish. Chicken is very versatile and most people like it.

If you were hosting an elegant dinner party, what would you serve?
I would try to work with seasonal/local ingredients. Even if the party is elegant, the food should still be kept simple. Simple food equals good food.

What are some of your favorite cookbooks?
La Covina Kristina • *The Joy of Cooking*.

If you're going to indulge, what's your food of choice?
Duck.

Do you have any tips for controlling food costs at home?
Look for coupons and family-size packaging.

Any final advice for the home cook?
Don't use recipes that require advanced skills.

What inspired you to become a chef?
Hanging on to my mother's and grandmother's coat strings when I was young, and later before school. I decided that I needed to expand my knowledge and skills, so I pursued Culinary and Pastry Arts degrees from Johnson & Wales University, in Providence, Rhode Island where I graduated in the top 1% of my class.

What kitchen tools do you recommend for the home cook?
Stainless steel mixing bowls • Maple rolling pin • Serrated, paring and French knives • Rubber spatula • Stainless steel whisk • Good measuring tools • Food processor.

What kitchen utensil or tool do you not have but would like to receive as a gift?
A ricer.

What are the most important techniques for the home cook to master?
I don't believe that you need to "master" any. But, to have a good, basic understanding of many techniques is essential – poaching, grilling, sautéing, basting, pan frying, braising, dicing, various knife cuts and a proper understanding of the equipment each technique uses.

Do you have any humorous anecdotes, either from your home or professional kitchen?
On Christmas Day, my grandmother and brother were sitting together. She had made Charlotte Russe for dessert. When I was helping to clean up from dinner and serve dessert, I saw a pound of whipped butter and noticed that it was the same color as the "Russe" custard. I formed ladyfingers around the butter, topped it with a cherry and served that to my brother and the Charlotte Russe to my grandmother. They both took large bites. My grandmother asked, "Isn't this wonderful?" All my brother could do was smile and nod his head.

What are some of the most common mistakes made by home cooks?
I believe that the most important thing is to have all of your ingredients on hand before preparation. And, allow yourself enough time to complete whatever you're making. Most mistakes are made by rushing your preparation and not having all the ingredients, or a proper substitution.

If a snoopy neighbor were to look in your home refrigerator today, what would he find?
Mineral water • Henry Baines Sauce • Black raspberry jam • Smoked Gouda cheese • Pommery mustard • Gold pineapple • Vidalia onions • Genoa salami • Pastrami • Chardonnay • Something moldy and unidentifiable in a small container in the back.

What's your favorite style of entertaining?
Any alfresco dining. We love to entertain outdoors on our massive deck – "hot tub parties" with simple buffets, lots of grilling.
Most of our parties are informal, except around the holidays, and then it's fine china, crystal and silver formal place settings.

If you're cooking for family or close friends, what are some of your favorite dishes to serve?
Grilled beef, pork, or chicken simply marinated; pico de gallo; fresh baked breads; stuffed pastas, such as tortellini, ravioli, and agnolotti.; grilled veggies; and sinfully rich desserts with simple presentations.

If you were hosting an elegant dinner party, what would you serve?
Grilled shrimp or shellfish, such as Oysters Rockefeller; crisp green salad with sliced fruit, such as apple or pear, roasted nuts and a rich savory cheese, such as Maytag Blue; potatoes any way, probably Duchess; a duet entrée of stuffed beef tenderloin with a rich Chianti sauce, and fresh fish (John Dory) with sautéed sorrel and a beurre blanc sauce; simple oven roasted vegetables; and probably a cheesecake, Bananas Foster, or white chocolate Amaretto mousse.

What are some of your favorite cookbooks?
Party Food, by Lorna Wing • *The Fine Art of Delectable Desserts,* by Camille Glenn • *Cocktail Food,* by Barber and Whiteford • *Mastering the Art of French Cooking,* by Julia Child and Simone Beck • *The Antipasto Table,* by Michele Scicolone

If you're going to indulge, what's your food of choice?
Home made gelato, any caramel dessert, Modjeska candy and baklava.

Any final advice for the home cook?
Don't be afraid to experiment. Create your own recipes. • Have fun when you cook!

What inspired you to become a chef?

When I came to America, I saw the respect a professional chef received. I had the training and gift to be a chef and decided to pursue the career.

What kitchen tools do you recommend for the home cook?

A nice, thick wooden (preferably antique) cutting board • Good chefs' knives

What kitchen utensil or tool do you not have but would like to receive as a gift?

It's not really a kitchen tool, but I can wish, right? So, I'd say a wine cellar.

What is one of the most important techniques for the home cook to master?

To learn to not overcook anything.

What are some common mistakes made by home cooks?

Overcooking and using wrong temperatures.

If a snoopy neighbor were to look in your home refrigerator today, what would he find?

Chinese food leftovers, Mountain Dome sparkling wine, Spam and other potted meats (yes, it's true), Kalamata olives and farm eggs.

What's your favorite style of entertaining?

Sit-down dinners. I don't drink, so I like this style of entertaining because the emphasis is on the food.

If you're cooking for family or close friends, what are some of your favorite dishes to serve?

Salbutes, traditional small tortillas topped with a variety of ingredients • Ojaldra, ham and cheese stuffed phyllo pastry.

If you were hosting an elegant dinner party, what would you serve?

Fresh hammer head shark served seaside.

What are some of your favorite cookbooks?

All of Diane Kennedy's Mexican cookbooks • Old French cookbooks • Other antique cookbooks.

If you're going to indulge, what's your food of choice?

Fresh lobster ceviche, burning hot with habanero peppers, served with totopo chips.

Do you have any tips for controlling food costs at home?

When refrigerating foods, be sure they are wrapped carefully to reduce spoilage.

Any final advice for the home cook?

Yes. Come eat at the Mayan Gypsy. Forget cooking at home!

What inspired you to become a chef?
Fate and a family of women who loved to cook. I paid attention.

What kitchen tools do you recommend for the home cook?
A good set of knives! • Food processor • The best pots and pans you can afford • Spatula • Tongs • Whisk • Butcherblock cutting board • Your own two hands.

What kitchen utensil or tool do you not have but would like to receive as a gift?
A wood burning pizza oven.

What are some important techniques for the home cook to master?
Knife skills • Organization • Heat regulation.

Do you have any humorous cooking anecdotes, either from your home or professional kitchen?
I once had an employee who was looking for the canned tuna. It was literally right in front of her. I walked over and put my finger on the can. She looked really confused, then responded with, "But, that says "Chicken of the Sea" on it." I still laugh at that one!

What are some common mistakes made by home cooks?
Being too dependent on recipes and taking recipes too literally. • Being afraid of making mistakes. Making mistakes teaches great lessons.

If a snoopy neighbor were to look in your home refrigerator today, what would he find?
Chinese condiment packages, milk, pickles, water and carry-out containers.

If you're cooking for family or close friends, what are some of your favorite dishes to serve?
Comfort food.

If you were hosting an elegant dinner party, what would you serve?
It would depend on the season. You wouldn't serve cassoulet in the middle of summer.

What are some of your favorite cookbooks?
Out of Kentucky Kitchens, by Marion Flexner • Antique cookbooks.

If you're going to indulge, what's your food of choice?
Sushi.

Do you have any tips for controlling food costs at home?
Be creative with leftovers.

Any final advice for the home cook?
Don't be afraid to experiment. Trust your instincts.

What inspired you to become a chef?

Although I cooked all through high school, the thought of it being a "serious career" never dawned on me until my dad threatened, "You'd better get motivated about something or we're shipping you off to the Navy." The rest just kind of came naturally.

What kitchen tools do you recommend for the home cook?

As with all other aspects of cooking, keep it simple:
• A sharp knife and a steel to keep it sharp
• Cutting board • Large mixing bowl • Whisk • Rubber spatula • Metal spatula • Nice heavy skillet
• Thick bottom sauce pot (nothing fancy, just the basics – your fancy, non-stick sauté pan should almost never be used).

What kitchen utensil or tool do you not have but would like to receive as a gift?

A fine mesh metal strainer.

What are some of the most important techniques for the home cook to master?

Timing, so that all the food on the table is hot
• Taste, season, taste, season, taste, taste, taste.

Any humorous cooking anecdotes, either from your home or professional kitchen?

It's always fun to see how fast the servers will eat spoonfuls of cold fat when it is presented like ice cream.

What are some of the most common mistakes made by home cooks?

Not tasting • Having too much faith in a recipe can cause people to ignore common sense.

If a snoopy neighbor were to look in your home refrigerator today, what would he find?

Too much left over carry-out. • At least four different hot sauces

What's your favorite style of entertaining?

Barbecues/pot luck. It seems the most enjoyable meals are the ones enjoyed by all the people who prepared them together.

If you're cooking for family or close friends, what are some of your favorite dishes to serve?

Gumbo, ribs, twice baked potatoes and margaritas.

If you were hosting an elegant dinner party, what would you serve?

The menu would be based on the highest quality products available to me that day at the markets.

What is one of your favorite cookbooks?

The Joy of Cooking.

If you're going to indulge, what are your foods of choice?

Fried chicken and ice cream.

Any final advice for the home cook?

Decide "what's for dinner" at the market based on what's fresh or what suits your mood.

What inspired you to become a chef?

I grew up outside of New York City and was always exposed to wonderful food. I think I have an obsession for great food. To see the joy it brings to people means so much. Food makes people happy. Food can be comforting or sensuous.

What kitchen tools do you recommend for the home cook?

Good knives • Whisks • A KitchenAid mixer • A Cuisinart food processor • A high quality sauté pan • Heavy gauge pots.

What are the most important techniques for the home cook to master?

• Learning to follow recipes • Knowing all measurements and how to convert them, such as how to convert cups to weight • Knowing your oven's true temperature. Use a thermometer to check it.

Any humorous anecdotes, either from your home or professional kitchen?

Let me just say this: never put obstacles in the middle of your workspace. One might fall head first into a chocolate cake. We won't talk anymore about it.

What are some common mistakes made by home cooks?

Not cooking food long enough • Using too high a temperature and overcooking on the outside.

If a snoopy neighbor were to look in your home refrigerator today, what would he find?

Soy milk, salsa, several types of mustards, eggs, vegetarian hot dogs and, yes, chicken nuggets for the children.

What's your favorite style of entertaining?

It depends on the crowd and occasion. Usually I like buffets because they allow people to mingle. And, the hostess is not getting up and down as much as during a sit-down dinner.

If you're cooking for family or close friends, what are some of your favorite dishes to serve?

Matzo ball soup • A great lasagna.

If you were hosting an elegant dinner party, what would you serve?

An appetizer of smoked salmon and trout with capers; blue cheese and prosciutto bruschetta; crab cakes with rémoulade; a Bibb Quattro Fromaggio salad; halibut with pomegranates in a light orange beurre blanc; a cranberry sorbet for intermezzo; and a light and crispy layered raspberry phyllo dessert.

What is one of your favorite cookbooks?

Lenotre's Desserts and Pastries, by Gaston Lenotre.

If you're going to indulge, what's your food of choice?

Scallops.

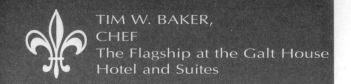

What inspired you to become a chef?
I love to cook and eat. It is a very creative job. And, I love working with food.

What kitchen tools do you recommend for the home cook?
Always purchase the best quality you can afford. You must have sharp knives. • I recommend a simple large Cuisinart. You don't need one with all the bells and whistles. • I love my Dutch oven and cast iron skillets.

What kitchen utensil or tool do you not have but would like to receive as a gift?
An emulsion blender.

What general advice do you have for the home cook?
Develop good knife skills • Don't overcook your food • Practice simplicity • Always use the freshest food possible.

What are some of the most common mistakes made by home cooks?
Overcooking • Not seasoning enough – or over-seasoning.

If a snoopy neighbor were to look in your home refrigerator today, what would he find?
Mostly condiments. Truffle oil • 8 different kinds of mustard • Baby Formula • Veuve Cliquot Champagne • Beer • Kale greens • Daikon.

What's your favorite style of entertaining?
Grilling out with friends because it's casual and fun.

If you're cooking for family or close friends, what are some of your favorite dishes to serve?
Home-style comfort food, such as grilled pork chops, mashed potatoes, country style green beans, kale greens and black-eyed peas.

If you were hosting an elegant dinner party, what would you serve?
Beef tenderloin, asparagus, goat cheese scalloped potatoes, and a trifle.

What are some of your favorite cookbooks?
The Dean & Deluca Cookbook • Anything by Alice Waters, Alfred Portale or Rick Bayless

If you're going to indulge, what's your food of choice?
Sushi or lobster.

Do you have any tips for controlling food costs at home?
Learn creative ways to use leftovers. • Cook one-pot meals. They also save time.

Any final advice for the home cook?
Learn from your mistakes • Don't be afraid to experiment • Cook what you love.

What inspired you to become a chef?

I remember playing with my sister Nancy's *Susie Bake Oven*, but at around the age of 12, my parents enrolled me in the State University of New York's School of Circus Arts, where I flourished. I then joined some traveling circus troupes. My side job was moving animal cages. But, due to my age and size, they decided to place me with the cook.

What kitchen tools do you recommend for the home cook?

(A sharp knife, no matter what brand or price. A lot of people like stainless steel knives because they keep an edge longer. However, they are generally harder to sharpen than carbon steel knives. Carbon steel sharpens easily but these knives loose their edge more quickly. They also tend to rust. • A good pepper mill that has an adjustable grind feature. In my home kitchen I have two – one for white pepper and one for black pepper. • For pots, the heavier the better. I believe heavy pots offer better versatility, heat more evenly and are generally easier to clean. • Always keep two types of whisks on hand: a stiff one for items such as spaetzle and thicker type batters, and a piano wire whisk for whipping things such as Hollandaise sauce and egg whites. • Although wooden cutting boards require more thorough cleaning and delicate care than cutting boards made of other materials, they not only give a better look to your kitchen, but they also tend to be much more forgiving to your knives' edges as well. • Another gadget that I find comes in handy is the mortar and pestle. I use it to hand-grind rubs for meats and make homemade mustards. I purchased mine in an art studio in Maine. It's hand carved and made of the most beautiful olive wood.

What kitchen utensil or tool do you not have but would like to receive as a gift?

Honestly, I think I have at least one of every tool and/or gadget that is made or needed to run a successful home kitchen. In fact, just the other day, I purchased a second quail egg topper (as if one isn't enough). This scissor-like gadget is designed to snip off the tops of very small quail eggs.

What is the most important technique for the home cook to master?

Planning is everything!

What are home cooks' most common mistakes and how can they be avoided?

Not reading the recipe before they start cooking. It's very important to read through the entire recipe. • Also, not gathering everything that you'll need to prepare it. Include both the food and the equipment required for the dish or meal that you will be preparing. We call that mise en place. • Cooking should not be forced. It should flow as if it were your sixth sense. If it doesn't, please support your favorite local restaurant by making reservations!

If a snoopy neighbor were to look in your home refrigerator today, what would he find?

A couple dozen types of Asian condiments and spices, including Lap Chow, a type of dried Chinese sausage. Other than that, he'd find lots of vegetables, unsweetened iced jasmine tea, and fat free milk. Rarely will you ever see leftovers.

What's your favorite style of entertaining?

At home, I like to cook outside. Our last barbeque was a farewell one with our neighbors in New Jersey, before we moved to Louisville.

If you're cooking for family or close friends, what are some of your favorite dishes to serve?

The menu at the farewell barbeque consisted of some of my favorite things, such as Manila clams with fermented black beans, grilled Maine lobsters basted with garlic and extra virgin olive oil, grilled stuffed artichokes, and barbequed asparagus and eggplant. One time I served 7" Porterhouse steaks with 3' crab legs. Two steaks were enough to feed 20 or more guests. That was a meal to remember!

If you were hosting an elegant dinner party, what would you serve?

A wide variety of finger foods.

What are some of your favorite cookbooks?

The ones that have recipes that work! Far too often, a cookbook is beautiful but the recipes just don't work or the ingredients are unavailable.

If you're going to indulge, what's your food of choice?

I like everything from the Far East or Eastern Europe. (If you must know, my favorite thing to eat is my mother's Cinnamon Swirl Sour Cream Bundt Cake.)

Any final advice for the home cook?

Eat out more often!

What inspired you to become a chef?
I grew up cooking. It's rewarding. I love to do it. And, I get paid to do something I love.

What kitchen tools do you recommend for the home cook?
Hand grater • Burr mixer • Coffee grinder.

What kitchen utensil or tool do you not have but would like to receive as a gift?
A mandoline.

What is one of the most important techniques for the home cook to master?
Sauce making.

What are home cooks' most common mistakes?
Over salting • Walking away from an open flame or a skillet with grease • Overheating oils.

If a snoopy neighbor were to look in your home refrigerator today, what would he find?
Milk • Sundried tomatoes • Limes • Leftovers • Beer.

What's your favorite style of entertaining?
I prefer sit-down dinners because you can be more creative.

If you're cooking for family or close friends, what are some of your favorite dishes to serve?
Crusted Standing Pork Roast • Stuffings • Garlic Mashed Potatoes • Stuffed Mushrooms • Sea Bass Salad with Asian Vinaigrette

If you were hosting an elegant dinner party, what would you serve?
Cold Curry Carrot Soup • Blackened Soft-shell Crab with an Oyster Sauce Over Soba Noodles • Bibb and Brie Salad with Mandarin Oranges, Brie, Spicy Pecans and a Champagne Vinaigrette • Porcini Crusted Filet of Beef with A Red Wine Demi Glace served with Purple Peruvian Mashed Potatoes and Fresh Green Beans Garni • White Chocolate and Raspberry Torte

What are some of your favorite cookbooks?
Art Culinaire • *Saveur* Cookbooks (and magazine) • All of Emeril Lagasse's cookbooks.

If you're going to indulge, what's your food of choice?
Italian.

Do you have any tips for controlling food costs at home?
Shop around before you buy.

Any final advice for the home cook?
Don't give up if a recipe fails the first time; keep trying.

What inspired you to become a chef?
Pure and simple: a love of great food, lovingly prepared.

What kitchen tools do you recommend for the home cook?
Baking stone • A good, sturdy mixer.

What is one of the most important techniques for the home cook to master?
Patience.

Do you have any humorous anecdotes from either your professional or home kitchen?
An employee once handed me egg shells when I asked him for egg whites. Live and learn.

If a snoopy neighbor were to look in your home refrigerator today, what would he find?
Organic market veggies • Various cheeses • Countless mustards • Spring water.

What's your favorite style of entertaining?
Slow, enjoyable time with friends that can combine sit-down dinners, cocktail parties or buffets.

If you're cooking for family or close friends, what are some of your favorite dishes to serve?
Artisan pizzas or a tagine.

If you were hosting an elegant dinner party, what would you serve?
I would create a theme. Something seasonal, elegant and easy.

What are some of your favorite cookbooks?
Vegeterian Cooking for Everyone, by Deborah Madison • Any of the Moosewood cookbooks • And I love magazines.

If you're going to indulge, what's your food of choice?
Cereal • Chocolate • Cashews and almonds.

Do you have any tips for controlling food costs at home?
Go to the market daily • Be creative and use what's in your fridge.

Any final advice for the home cook?
Confidence is the key.

What inspired you to become a chef?

I was first inspired by watching my grandmother in the kitchen. I have had an interest in cooking since I was a child.

What kitchen tools do you recommend for the home cook?

Chinois (a fine mesh strainer) • Food mill • Cast iron skillet

What kitchen utensil or tool do you not have but would like to receive as a gift?

A Cameron Smoker Cooker.

What is one of the most important techniques for the home cook to master?

Braising.

What are some of the most common mistakes made by home cooks?

Not using real butter • Overcooking meats and pasta • Not cooking with the seasons.

If a snoopy neighbor were to look in your home refrigerator today, what would he find?

Rack of venison, a bottle of Sauvignon Blanc, European butter and a tarte Tatin.

What's your favorite style of entertaining?

Sit-down dinners. I prefer this style because you can show off or impress to any degree. I believe a dinner party should be an experience to remember, as well as a social event.

If you're cooking for family or close friends, what are some of your favorite dishes to serve?

Any wild game, such as venison and wild turkey. I also like to serve chocolate mousse cake with any buttercream.

If you were hosting an elegant dinner party, what would you serve?

It would depend on the people and the season. If they had a sophisticated palate, I would serve foie gras, Kumamoto oysters on the half shell, and Alaskan sablefish, if available.

What are some of your favorite cookbooks?

Chez Panise Desserts • *The French Professional Pastry Series.*

If you're going to indulge, what are your foods of choice?

Mediterranean foods, fresh seafood, foie gras, duck and sushi.

Do you have any tips for controlling food costs at home?

Buy only what you're going to cook a week at a time. • Don't forget about the crisper – you know, that box in your fridge with the vegetables that always go bad.

Any final advice for the home cook?

Don't give up after the first try. It should take more than one time to master something, especially desserts.

What inspired you to become a chef?
My mother was a gourmet cook and a great inspiration.

What kitchen tools do you recommend for the home cook?
A good quality chef's knife, either Henckels or Wüsthof. • Some great cookbooks, such as *The New Joy of Cooking*, by Irma S. Rombauer; any of the Moosewood cookbooks; *The Cake Bible*, by Rose Levy Beranbaum • And, a terrific food reference book, *The Food Lovers' Companion*.

What kitchen utensil or tool do you not have but would like to receive as a gift?
A propane torch for brûlées.

What are some of the most important techniques for the home cook to master?
Basic knife skills • Knowing and then controlling the temperature of your oven and range top.

What is one of the most common mistakes made by home cooks?
Not reading the recipe completely before beginning to cook.

If a snoopy neighbor were to look in your home refrigerator today, what would he find?
Lots and lots of condiments, such as chipotle sauce, Tabasco, Texas Pete, soy sauce, Rooster sauce, garlic chile sauce, sweet chile sauce, ketchup and several different mustards.

What's your favorite style of entertaining?
I like formal dinners. It's just fun to play dress up every now and again. I also like barbecues because you can slow everything down, talk and enjoy a beverage or two.

If you're cooking for family or close friends, what is one of your favorite dishes to serve?
Something smoked, such as a brisket or baby back ribs.

If you were hosting an elegant dinner party, what would you serve?
Pâté de foie gras, cornichons, goat cheese and assorted crackers; standing rib roast with horse-radish whipped potatoes, Yorkshire pudding, and haricots vert; and a chocolate soufflé with vanilla ice cream.

What are some of your favorite cookbooks?
In addition to those I've already mentioned, I especially like all of Paul Prudhomme's cookbooks • *Mastering the Art of French Cooking, Vols. I and II*, by Julia Child; • any of Barbara Tropp's cookbooks • and anything by Marcella Hazan.

If you're going to indulge, what is your food of choice?
I'd go for a B.L.T. with Hellmann's mayo, fresh black pepper, Bibb lettuce, Boar's Head platter bacon, and a September-ripened tomato still warm from the sun; and several Corona Lites, extra cold!

Do you have any tips for controlling food costs at home?
Shop for dry goods in bulk • Buy produce several times a week.

Any final advice for the home cook?
For dinner parties, try to prepare as much as you can ahead of time, and prepare foods you know. Practice other culinary endeavors on your family. If things go wrong, calm down and order out. Everybody likes pizza or Chinese food.

What inspired you to become a chef?

My mother and Mimmo Caschino, the first chef for whom I worked.

What kitchen tools do you recommend for the home cook?

A large wooden spoon is a must for Italian cooking • Chef's fork • Chef's knife • Thick cutting board.

What kitchen utensil or tool do you not have but would like to receive as a gift?

I'd be very happy to receive a Cuisinart food processor.

What are the most important techniques for the home cook to master?

Proper adherence to recipes • Knowledge of how to use the correct utensils • A patience for cooking

Would you like to share any professional hints?

• Use a large plate when serving an appetizer, even if the appetizer is small. It makes a better presentation. • Don't cover pastas or other entrees with too much sauce. • When serving a sauce with a dessert, use a sauce with a contrasting color.

Any humorous anecdotes from your professional or home kitchen?

When I first began working in a kitchen as a boy, I was watching the chef prepare a sauce. When I asked him how he made the sauce and how many eggs he used, he wouldn't tell me because he didn't want to share the secret recipe. So, after he left, I counted the eggshells in the trash. I later approached him and told him the number of eggs he had used. He couldn't believe I had gotten it right! I never told him my secret so that I could continue to find out what went into the dishes.

What are home cooks' most common mistakes?

Overcooking • Improper seasoning. • The best way to avoid cooking mistakes is to have a real love for good food. Then, you can learn how great food should taste.

If a snoopy neighbor were to look in your home refrigerator today, what would he find?

Milk, fruit and cheese. You must always have milk!

What's your favorite style of entertaining?

I have to say sit-down dinners. Because they are more intimate than cocktail parties or buffets, you're better able to carry on a conversation with your guests.

If you're cooking for family or close friends, what are some of your favorite dishes to serve?

It's very difficult to say what my favorite dishes are because I love so many. Also, I try to use seasonal ingredients as much as possible, so what's available would help determine what I serve. When planning the menu, I would think a lot about what each of the guests would like, then create dishes for them.

If you were hosting an elegant dinner party, what would you serve?

I'd splurge a bit and serve caviar, risotto, aragosta (lobster) and capretto (lamb).

What are some of your favorite cookbooks?

Sicilia in Bocca, by Antonio Lardella • *The Silver Spoon,* by Antonio Monti Tedeschi.

If you're going to indulge, what are your foods of choice?

Caviar and lamb.

Do you have any tips for controlling food costs at home?

Buy only what you need. • And, utilize all leftovers.

Any final advice for the home cook?

Try to prepare food that stores well. • And, always use fresh, fresh, fresh ingredients.

What inspired you to become a chef?

I was inspired by my parents' love of entertaining and travel. Also, I was greatly influenced by the food loving community in which I grew up.

What kitchen tools do you recommend for the home cook?

Good sharp knives • All-Clad stainless cookware • Salt and pepper mills • Chinese steamer • Griddle • Long and short tongs • Japanese mandoline • Dedicated spice mill • Burr (hand) blender.

What kitchen utensil or tool do you not have but would like to receive as a gift?

A tagine.

What are the most important techniques for the home cook to master?

Knife skills • Timing • Passion • And a bit of advice: If you really mess up the dinner, order Take-out.

Any humorous cooking anecdotes, either from your home or professional kitchen?

One too many martinis can make for a regrettable dinner party.

Do you have any general advice for the home cook?

Do what you are comfortable with. • Practice new dishes on the family. • Always have a backup plan.

If a snoopy neighbor were to look in your home refrigerator today, what would he find?

Lots of condiments. And Champagne.

What's your favorite style of entertaining?

I enjoy all styles of entertaining – cocktail parties, buffets and sit down dinners – as long as they are casual and well planned.

If you're cooking for family or close friends, what are some of your favorite dishes to serve?

Tamales • Pot stickers • Spring Rolls • Grilled Anything • Grit Casserole • Seasonal Salads.

If you were hosting an elegant dinner party, what would you serve?

Appetizer: Mousseline of pike with Sauce Nantua with crisp littleneck clams;

Salad: Salad of baby mustard greens and other baby greens, roasted beets, Capriole Farms Goat Cheese with caramelized cippolini onions, and a simple grapeseed oil and Xeres vinegar dressing;

Entrée: Roasted loin of lamb with lamb jus finished with Amontillado sherry; Pommes Anna with fine herbs; and Brussels sprouts with walnuts and pancetta;

Dessert: Oeufs à la Neige

Cheese Course: A selection of artisanal cheeses; *Petits Fours.*

What are some of your favorite cookbooks?

Larousse Gastronomique; Herring's Guide to Classical and Modern Cuisine; The Barefoot Contessa; The James Beard New York Times Cook Book; Gotham, by Alfred Portale; and John Ash's and Ronni Lundy's books.

If you're going to indulge, what's your food of choice?

It depends on my mood and the season.

Do you have any tips for controlling food costs at home?

Plan a menu and buy only what you need. • Store food properly. • Experiment with leftovers.

Any final advice for the home cook?

Fear not the kitchen. • Entertain friends and family with great passion. • Enjoy the pleasures of the table.

Pairing Food and Wine

Pairing food and wine can be a daunting, challenging and intimidating task. John Johnson, owner of The Wine Rack, in Louisville, shares his experience and insight on the multi-faceted subject of food and wine pairing.

10 Easy Rules to Wine and Food Bliss

Rule #1 - Enjoy!

Drink wine you actually like. If you simply cannot enjoy a Riesling (even dry), it doesn't matter how well it goes with spicy Asian food and curry. There are thousands of wines out there. My simple motto is to drink what you like, but don't be afraid to try something new once in a while.

Rule #2 - Special Wines for Wine Tastings

For serious wine tasting, the wines should be paired with simple foods or served on their own. Have plenty of water on hand and perhaps some simple French bread or plain crackers to refresh the palate and absorb some of the alcohol. But, let the wines have the spotlight.

Rule #3 - Cooking Technique Matters

How the food is prepared plays a role in wine selection. Chicken is perhaps the best example of this. Forget the "white meat means white wine" rule. Chicken breasts sautéed with lemon and parsley will go best with crisp white wine. However, grilled or roasted chicken goes just as nicely with a Pinot Noir or Côtes du Rhône. Without getting overly complicated, when the cooking technique itself adds more flavors to the food (as a charcoal grill does), select a red or a fuller-bodied white such as oaky Chardonnay.

Rule #4 - Other Ingredients

What other ingredients are on the plate? Seldom does anyone eat a piece of fish or turkey on its own. What accompanies the main item, as well as the spices and sauces used, should also be considered. It is often the case that the sauce will dominate the overall taste of the dish while side items tend to enhance. Thanksgiving dinner, for example, is usually served with a plethora of other tasty items. Why focus on just the turkey? When a feast of that magnitude is on, that's all the more reason to drink what you really love.

Rule #5 - Sweetness

As a good rule of thumb, the sweeter the food, the sweeter the wine should be. Sweet desserts will make whatever wine you sip following it taste less sweet and can come across as bitter. Alleviate this problem by serving a wine that is sweeter than the food. Even if you're not a fan of sweet wines, you may be surprised at how much you enjoy a Late Harvest Sauternes Semillon with Crème Brûlée.

Rule #6 - Fat

Fat will coat your mouth and make tannic wines, such as Cabernets, seem less astringent. This is why a full-bodied red goes better with a steak or piece of sharp cheddar cheese than it does on its own or with something such as trout. This principle is perhaps best applied toward fish. An oily, darker fleshed fish can go nicely with Pinot Noir while a flaky, delicate fish should be served with a white wine, such as Muscadet or Sauvignon Blanc. One word of caution: if you cook your steak until well done, much of the fat will be cooked off and, therefore, the wine's tannic qualities will increase. This is another reason to serve a good steak the way it tastes best – rare!

Rule #7 - Acidity

Foods high in acidity will decrease the perception of sourness in wine and therefore make it taste more mellow. A good rule to use is that for highly acidic foods, serve higher acidity wines, such as Sauvignon Blancs or Rieslings.

Rule #8 - Salt

Salt decreases tannic reactions. It's yet another reason, along with the fat involved, why the full bodied reds of the world (Cabernet Sauvignon, Zinfandel, Barolo, Bordeaux) can go so well with intense blue cheeses like Roquefort.

Rule #9 - Body

The heartier the food, the fuller the wine. This principle applies equally to red and white wines.

Rule #10 - Aroma

Aroma plays a role. Aromatic foods - those with herbal ingredients, and garlic and butter are enhanced by aromatic wines.

FOOD FOR THOUGHT

I know I've just given you a lot of guidelines to use. Don't worry. If you start to feel overwhelmed when considering these factors while shopping for a bottle or two of wine, just focus on the food characteristics that stand out most. If you still feel anxious, refer first and foremost to Rule #1 - Enjoy!

Additional consideration: Think country of origin. The civilizations of the three primary European wine producers (Italy, France and Spain) have been enjoying food and wine together for eons. I firmly believe that dishes from these wine-producing countries do indeed go better with wines from the same regions. This is not a firm rule but a useful tip.

When you're ready to select wines for specific types of food, think about these general categories:

Beef and Lamb

This is an easy one. Think medium to full-bodied reds (Merlot, Cabernet Sauvignon, Northern Rhone (Syrah), Pinot Noir, Chianti) and you will do just fine. Things to watch for are the fattiness or leanness of beef. Remember: higher fat levels permit more tannins in the wine. Also for beef stew fans, you may want to go with a more youthful red such as Zinfandel or Shiraz from Australia with nice fruity qualities to help cut the richness of the stew.

Pork

Ahh, the other white meat. Pork is versatile and goes well with many reds and whites. Focus on the method of cooking and the spices involved. One of my favorite dishes is Pork Tenderloin roasted with a mix of rosemary, salt, pepper, garlic and whole black peppercorns. The peppercorns clash with tannic reds and make off-dry whites like Johannisberg Riesling a better match. If choosing a red, leaner pork goes better with medium-bodied reds such as a Spanish Monastrel while a pork roast with more fat can handle fuller reds such as Bordeaux.

Poultry

This is a broad area. First, remember the cooking method tips from the previous section. Second, the wilder the bird, the redder the wine. Game birds such as quail and pheasant have stronger flavors and are terrific with Cabernet, Primitivo, Grenache and Barbaresco. Wine for chicken depends primarily on how the chicken is cooked. Domestic duck and goose go well with richer white wines. Wild duck and goose pair better with red. For turkey, think fruity reds like Zins, Beaujolais or whites such as Rieslings and Chardonnay.

Fish and Shellfish

Overall, you are safer with white wines like Muscadet, Sauvignon Blancs, Semillons and Chardonnays. However, if you are having an oily fish, try a red of light to medium weight (Pinot Noir or a nice Côtes du Rhône). Smoked fish goes well with aromatic whites such as those from the Alsace region of France and crisp acidic Sancerre wines. Also, with shellfish such as lobster and crab, consider the serving temperature. These foods served cold go better with sweeter white wines, but served hot are a better mate for a Chardonnay.

Pasta

Having been professionally taught to cook Italian and French cuisine, I have a deep respect for the myriad ways pasta can be prepared. It always irks me to see the phrase "goes well with pasta" on the back of a wine label. This is indeed a massive over simplification. In the interest of time, focus on the ingredients of the sauce. Pasta with a pesto sauce goes best with an aromatic white wine such as Sauvignon Blanc or Pinot Grigio. Most red sauces go well with classic Italian reds like Valpolicella, Chianti, or Barbera. Seafood and Alfredo based pastas are best served with Pinot Grigio, Sauvignon Blanc or unoaked Chardonnay and Gavi.

Asian and Mexican

I grouped these together for one simple reason: spiciness. There is one other common thread in that neither region makes wine. For spicy Asian, go with a contrast. A Pinot Gris with a touch of sweetness or an off-dry Riesling do the job well for whites. For reds, beware of tannins and spicy reds such as Australian Shiraz. Hot spicy foods cause a reaction known as chemesthesis in the mouth, which basically means that the spiciness of the food sensitizes your palate. When you take a sip of wine following a bite, at first the wine may seem fruitier, but after a while the cumulative heat from the food builds and that same wine will seem more tannic and peppery. This makes me feel like there is a campfire in my mouth, which I generally try to avoid. So, with reds choose a smooth and easy Merlot or light Pinot Noir. For non-spicy Asian food, Chardonnay and Gewürztraminer tend to be good bets.

For Mexican food, drink beer. It truly is the best match for those peppers and spices. If you really feel like wine, go with a light-bodied red.

Desserts

Just remember the sweeter the food, the sweeter the wine. Late harvest Rieslings and Sauternes style Semillon wines affected by Botrytis have a wonderful combination of sweetness and fruit which compliment most desserts. A note on chocolate: Slightly bitter chocolates are an easy match for California Cabernets, Merlots and French Bordeaux. If the chocolate is sweeter, go with sweeter wines. Ruby Port also makes a nice pairing with milk chocolate, especially on a cold winter night.

Apéritifs

Sparkling wines are a good way to get a dinner party going. In addition to Champagne, think of fruity Prosecco as well. Rosé and Pinot Grigio are also nice, especially in summer.

The amount and complexity of information available regarding food and wine pairing may seem overwhelming. But, like anything, the more you learn and try, the easier and more fun wine and food pairing becomes. I believe that learning about wine and applying a few simple guidelines to food and wine pairing will help make your culinary journey through life more pleasurable.

Mr. Johnson is a graduate of the Cook Street School of Fine Cooking, in Denver, and is also designated by the International Wine Guild as a Certified Sommelier and Certified Chef of Wine Arts.

About The Restaurants

You will find this guide helpful the next
time you dine in a Louisville restaurant.

Artemesia
620 E. Market Street
Louisville, KY 40202
583-4177
• Contemporary Continental Cuisine

Asiatique
106 Sears Avenue
Louisville, KY 40207
899-3578
• Pacific Rim Fusion Cuisine

August Moon Chinese Bistro
2269 Lexington Road
Louisville, KY 40206
502-456-6569
• Contemporary Chinese Cusine with a
  Malaysian flair

Avalon
1314 Bardstown Road
Louisville, KY 40204
502-454-5336
• Fresh American Cuisine with an
  emphasis on comfort foods

Azalea Restaurant
3612 Brownsboro Road
Louisville, KY 40207
895-5493
• New American Cuisine

Baxter Station Bar and Grill
1201 Payne Street
Louisville, KY 40204
502-584-1635
• American Bistro

Bristol Bar and Grille
1321 Bardstown Road
502-456-1702
300 N. Hurstbourne Parkway
502-426-0627
• Continental Cuisine

Buck's
425 W. Ormsby Street
Louisville, KY 40203
502-637-5284
• Continental Cuisine

Café Metro
1700 Bardstown Road
Louisville, KY 40205
502-458-4830
• Continental Cuisine

Club Grotto American Bistro
2116 Bardstown Road
Louisville, KY 40205
502-459-5275
• Eclectic, simple cuisine with an emphasis
  on fresh seafood and seasonal produce

El Mundo
2345 Frankfort Avenue
Louisville, KY 40206
502-899-9930
• Fresh, Eclectic Mexican Cuisine

The English Grill
in The Camberley Brown Hotel
Fourth Street and Broadway
Louisville, KY 40202
502-583-1234
• New American Cuisine with a
  Strong Regional Accent

Equus
122 Sears Avenue
Louisville, KY 40207
502-897-9721
• American Regional Cuisine

Greek Paradise Café
1605 Story Avenue
Louisville, KY 40206
502-595-7222
• Greek Cuisine

Jack Fry's Restaurant
1007 Bardstown Road
Louisville, KY 40204
502-452-9244
• New American Bistro Cuisine

Jicama Grill
1538 Bardstown Road
Louisville, KY 40205
502-454-4383
• Contemporary Latin Cuisine

Le Relais
2817 Taylorsville Road
Bowman Field
Louisville, KY 40205
502-451-9020
• French Cuisine

Lilly's and La Pêche
1147 Bardstown Road
Louisville, KY 40204
502-451-0447
• Eclectic, Seasonal Cuisine

Lynn's Paradise CafÈ
984 Baxter Avenue
Louisville, KY 40204
502-583-3447
• Home Cooking/Southern Cuisine

Porcini
2730 Frankfort Avenue
Louisville, KY 40206
502-894-8686
• Italian Cuisine

Restaurante The Mayan Gypsy
624 E. Market Street
Louisville, KY 40202
502-583-3300
• Tropical Intermex Cuisine

Salsa South Beach
2300 Frankfort Avenue
Louisville, KY 40206
502-897-3930
• Miami Fusion Cuisine

Shariat's
2901 Brownsboro Road
Louisville, KY 40206
502-899-7878
• Continental Cuisine

Steam---Fire & Ice
2427 Bardstown Road
Louisville, KY 40204
502-454-9944
• Contemporary Comfort Cuisine

Sweet Surrender
1416 Bardstown Road
Louisville, KY 40204
502-458-6363
• Distinctive European and American
  Desserts and Light Fare

The Flagship at
The Galt House Hotel and Suites
Fourth Avenue at the River
Louisville, KY 40202
502-589-5200
• Continental Cuisine

The Oakroom
at the Seelbach Hilton Louisville
500 S. Fourth Street
Louisville, KY 40202
502-585-3200
• New Regional Continental Cuisine

The Palmer Room
at Lake Forest Country Club
14000 Landmark Drive
Louisville, KY 40245
502-253-9352
• American Cuisine

The Patron Restaurant
3400 Frankfort Avenue
Louisville, KY 40207
• Modern American Cuisine

211 Clover Lane
211 Clover Lane
Louisville, KY 40207
• Continental Cuisine

Uptown Café
1624 Bardstown Road
Louisville, Kentucky 40205
• New American Cuisine with a Regional
  Twist

Vincenzo's
150 S. Fifth Street
Louisville, KY 40202
502-580-1350
• Italian Continental Cuisine

Winston's at Sullivan University
3101 Bardstown Road
Louisville, KY 40205
502-456-0980
• Global Cuisine with Regional Influences

INDEX

Achiote paste, 62

Adobo, 54

Aioli
    Cilantro Lime, 11

Almonds, 46

Apple
    caramelized, 3
    Cider glaze, 48
    Compote, 98
    Individual Fried Apple Cheesecakes, 78
    Sauce, 65

Appleton Rum, 99

Arugula , 37

Artichoke Fritters, 9

Asparagus: 53, 58, 72

Avocado
    Hummus, 6
    Tuna Tartare, 7
    and Goat Cheese Quesadilla, 13
    Shrimp Ceviche, 18

Bacon
    Applewood smoked: 30, 53
    Crab Garlic Custard on Organic Spinach
    with Warm Bacon Dressing, 20
    Wrapped Scallops: 12, 32

Baklava, 86

Banana, 102
    Caramel Cake, 93
    Chocolate and Banana Dacquoise, 99
    Chutncy, 63
    Poppyseed Guggelhopf, 82

Beans
    Black Bean and Meat Stew, 54
    Black Bean Cakes, 23
    Black Bean Chili, 21
    Fava, 57
    White bean relish, 27
    Bean paste marinade, 71

Beef
    Flank steak, 56
    Ground, 52
    Skirt steak, 56
    Tenderloin, 54

Beef Tenderloin Stuffed with Wild Mushrooms
and Goat Cheese, 43

Belgian Waffle De-Lite, 102

Beer and Chile Braised
Boneless Short Ribs, 42

Beets
    Roasted Yellow Beet Salad, 30

Beurre Blanc: 12, 19, 37

Bisque
    Tomato, 27

Blackberry Sauce, 87

Bocconcini Di Vitello, 73

Bok Choy: 39, 40

Bourbon: 15, 60, 80, 96
    Ball French Toast, 89
        Caramel, 92
        Chocolate Pecan Tart, 84
        Vanilla Custard, 89

Brie Salad, 8

Buttermilk Panna Cotta, 98

Cabbage
    Napa, 66

Cake
    Banana Caramel, 93

Calvados And Tarragon Pork Tenderloin
Medallions, 57

Cappuccino
    Peppered Wild Mushroom Cappuccino, 28

Caramel
    Banana Cake, 93
    Bourbon, 92

Ceviche
    Shrimp, 18

Cheese
    Smoked Gouda Corncakes, 72

Cheesecake
    Individual fried apple, 78
    Pumpkin, 88
    White Chocolate Pumpkin, 91

Chefs' Secrets, 103

Chicken, 44
    and Green Chili Wontons, 24
    Braised with Local Organic Mushrooms, 69
    General's Chicken, 41
    Kentuckian, 60
    Roast breast, 48

Chicken Stock, 17

Chili
    Black Bean, 21

Chipotle Basil cream sauce, 44

Rubbed Mahi Mahi, 51

Chocolate
    and Banana Dacquoise, 99
    Bourbon Chocolate Pecan Tart, 84
    Flourless Truffle Torte, 94
    Individual Chocolate Bombes, 101
    Orbit, 85
    White chocolate mousse, 87
    White Chocolate Mousse Torte, 94
    White Chocolate Pumpkin Cheesecake, 91

Churrascos De Argentina, 56

Chutney
    Banana, 63
    Mango Strawberry, 39

Clams
    Littleneck, 58
    Steamer Clams with Country Ham, 14

Coconut, 102
    Milk, 77

Coffee
    Malted Coffee Ice Cream, 96

Corn, 51
    Cakes, 72
    Fritters, 12

Cornbread
    Stuffing, 48

Crab, 16
    Garlic Custard, 20
    Tuna Tartare Napoleon, 7

Crab cakes
    Dungeness Crabcakes, 19
    Granchio Torcello, 22

Cranberries: 3, 8

Crème Anglaise, 94

Crème Brûlée with Fresh Raspberries, 100

Curry, 39

Custard
    Bourbon Vanilla, 89
    Crab Garlic, 20

Dacquoise
    Chocolate and Banana, 99

Duck Breast with Pomegranate Walnut Sauce, 64

Eggplant, 52
    Nests, 37
    Torte, 33

Escarole, 47

Farofa, 54

Feijoada, 54

Flan
    El Mundo's, 83

Fontina, 73

Frangelica, 82

French Bread Pudding with Bourbon Sauce, 80

French Toast
    Bourbon Ball, 89

Fritters
    Corn, 12

General's Chicken, 41

Goat Cheese: 43, 59
    Quesadillas, 13

Gouda
    Smoked Gouda corncakes, 72

Greens
    Kale or mustard, 54

Grits
    Creamy with Chevre, 59

Grouper
    Sautéed with Braised Napa Cabbage, 66

Guggelhopf, Banana Poppyseed, 82

Ham
    Country: 14, 50

Heavenlies, 97

Hominy, 50

Honeydew, 77

Hummus
    Avocado, 6

Ice Cream, 102
    Malted Coffee, 96

Italian Cream Cake, 90

Ketchup
    Raspberry, 71

Key Lime Pie, 81
    White Chocolate Mousse Torte with
    Blackberry Sauce, 87

Lamb
    Loin with Hominy Grits, 50
    Roasted Leg Stuffed with
    Wild Mushrooms, 47
    Roasted Rack, 67
    Slow-Roasted with Mediterranean Sauce, 59

Lobster
    Broth, 58
    Scallop-lobster tortellini, 37

Mahi Mahi: 37, 51

Malted Coffee Ice Cream, 96

Malaysian Style Tapioca Pearls
with Honeydew, 77

Mango, 102
    and strawberry chutney, 39
    salsa, 49

Maple and Walnut Risotto, 67

Marsala: 68, 74

Mojo de Ajo, 49

Moussaka, 52

Mousse
    Chocolate: 92, 101
    White chocolate torte: 87, 95

Mozzarella
    Fresh Mozzarella and Prosciutto Stuffed
    French Veal Chop, 68

Mushrooms, 44
    and root vegetable tartlets, 25
    Morel Marsala Sauce, 68
    Shitake soy glaze, 66
    Wild: 4, 32, 33, 40, 43, 47, 53, 69, 74
    Wild mushroom cappuccino, 28

Osso Bucco, 61

Oyster sauce, 74

Pandaisia, 16

Panko, 68

Panna Cotta
    Buttermilk, 98

Peaches and Cream, 79

Peapods, 74

Pear Semillon Coulis, 31

Pecans: 46, 84, 93

Peppered Wild Mushroom Cappuccino, 28

Phyllo dough, 86

Pico de Gallo, 54

Pineapple, 102

Pine nuts, 20

Pistachios: 8, 74
    Oil, 74

Pita bread: 6, 16

Pomegranate
    Walnut Sauce, 64

Poppyseeds
    Banana Poppyseed Guggelhopf, 82

Pork
    Chops and Apple Sauce, 65
    Jack Fry's Pork Chop, 53
    Loin Dijonaise, 45
    Rum marinated chop, 63

Tenderloin: 54, 57

Potatoes: 52, 53, 58
 Purple, 51
 Salad. 57

Prawns
 Roasted in Lobster Broth Reduction, 58
 Tempura fried, 11

Prosciutto, 73
 Stuffed veal chop, 68

Pudding
 French Bread, 80

Pumpkin
 White Chocolate Cheesecake, 91
 Cheesecake, 88

Quail
 Spicy Grilled, 71

Quesadillas, 13

Quince and apple compote, 98

Raspberries: 71, 100

Raspberry Ketchup, 71

Red Snapper
 Al Mojo de Ajo, 49

Restaurant Information, 143

Ribs
 Short ribs, 42

Rice: 54, 62, 67, 69

Risotto
 Maple walnut, 67

Rum
 Appleton, 99
 Marinated Pork Chop, 63

Rutabagas, 25

Salmon, 16
 Smoked, 10
 Spread, 26
 Tartare, 5
 Tikin Xik, 62

Salsa
 Mango, 49

Sauce
 Achiote (Annatto), 62
 Béchamel, 52
 Blackberry, 87

Sauce *(cont.)*
 Bourbon, 80
 Caramel apple. 78
 Chimichurri, 56
 Chipotle basil cream, 44
 Dijonaise, 45
 Espagnole, 61
 Ginger/Soy, 24
 Morel Marsala, 68
 Rémoulade: 9, 22
 Strawberry Garlic, 4

Sausage
 Andouille, 48
 Breakfast links, 54
 Chorizo: 51, 54
 Smoked links, 54

Scallops: 12, 32, 37
 Diver Scallops with Bibb Lettuce
 and Black Truffle Oil, 17

Sea Bass, 29

Seafood
 See individual seafood

Shortbread Cookie Crust, 87

Shrimp:15, 16, 33
 Ceviche, 18
 Madagascar, 34

Smoked Gouda Corncakes, 72

Spinach: 20, 34

Squash
 Butternut, 19

Stew
 Brazilian black bean and meat, 54

Strawberries and mango chutney, 39

Stuffing
 Andouille-Cornbread, 48

Syrup, maple, 67

Tacos, 49

Tahini, 6

Tapioca
 Malaysian Style Tapioca Pearls, 77

Tart
 Bourbon Chocolate Pecan, 84

Tartlets
    Root vegetable, 25
Tempura
    Fried Prawns with Blue Corneal and
    Cilantro Lime Aioli, 11
Tobiko, 5
Tomato Bisque, 27
Torte
    Eggplant, 33
    Flourless Truffle, 94
    White Chocolate Mousse, 95
Tortellini
    Scallop-lobster, 37
    Tri-colored with Chipotle Basil Cream
    Sauce, 44
Tortillas: 13, 49, 91
Tortilla Chips: 18, 91
Tortino Di Melenzane Con Risotto E
Funghetti Di Bosco, 33
Triple Sec, 79
Trout with Almond Four Dijonaise, 46
Truffle Oil, 17
Tuna Tartare Napoleon, 7

Veal
    Chop, stuffed with Mozzarella and
    Prosciutto, 68
    Osso Bucco, 61
    Roulade, 73
    Stir Fry of Veal with Enoki Mushrooms, 74
    Stock, 57
Vegetables
    (see individual vegetables)
    Root vegetable tartlets, 25
Vinaigrette
    Cranberry, 30
    Hazelnut, 29
    Raspberry, 8
Waffle
    Belgian, 102
Wahoo, 39
Walnuts: 67, 86, 97
Pomegranate walnut sauce, 64
Wines – Pairing Food and Wine, 139
Wontons, 74
    Green chili, 24
Zucchini, 71

NOTES

NOTES

NOTES

_____

_____

_____

_____

_____

_____

_____

_____

_____

_____

_____

_____

_____

_____

_____

_____

_____

_____

_____

_____

_____

NOTES

NOTES

NOTES

NOTES